Transforming Finance in the Age of AI

Transforming Finance in the Age of AI

A CFO's Guide to Implementing Intelligent Financial Systems

Daniel Villani

Published by Game Changer Publishing

Paperback ISBN: 978-1-969372-08-7

Hardcover ISBN: 978-1-969372-09-4

Digital ISBN: 978-1-969372-10-0

GC GAME CHANGER PUBLISHING

www.GameChangerPublishing.com

For Mia, Giulia, and Anthony

Follow your dreams and don't be afraid to take risks. I wasn't an entrepreneur until I started my first company. I wasn't an inventor until I filed my first patent. I wasn't an author until I wrote my first book. I almost wasn't any of those; fortunately, I set aside my (and others') limiting beliefs and took the risks, and I will always encourage you to do the same.

As hockey legend Wayne Gretzky said,
"You miss one hundred percent of the shots you don't take."

Read This First

As a special thank you for reading this book, we have
provided a link for you to download
our Data Quality Checklist.

If you purchased this book online and you've found this book
helpful, I'd appreciate it if you'd leave a review!

Transforming Finance in the Age of AI

A CFO's Guide to Implementing Intelligent Financial Systems

Daniel Villani

Contents

Introduction

Over the past eighteen years, I have worked with companies of all sizes and in numerous industries, implementing financial systems to help them build a competitive advantage and assisting them with automating tasks when it seemed impossible to do so. My experience has uniquely positioned me to help you transform your company as you look to implement your next-generation financial systems.

Why did I write this book? After consulting for more than forty companies across various industries, I began to notice recurring patterns. Many companies were sacrificing long-term performance for short-term gain without even realizing it. With the emergence of AI, these sacrifices were jeopardizing their chances of successful AI implementations.

Introduction

The purpose of this book is to raise awareness of the basic requirements for a successful AI implementation and what it truly means to be ready for AI. Although the concepts are universal, applicable to any company in any industry, I primarily wrote this book for CFOs and finance leaders who want to build the next generation of finance systems powered by AI.

The examples in this book draw from my eighteen-year career in technology and focus on the competitive advantages I have helped create for numerous companies. While many consultants claim to be innovative, few actually hold any real intellectual property. I have been awarded two U.S. patents for my automation and AI software, with additional patents pending in the United States, plus international patents pending in the European Union and Canada. Furthermore, I possess over seventy certifications, ranging from individual courses to certifications from top business and technology schools across the country. I don't teach "best practices" from twenty years ago; I constantly invest in cutting-edge technology and research to provide you with the most valuable insights.

I began my career in technology support. During that time, I learned what it takes to support enterprise clients and how many issues arise from shortcuts taken during implementations. For instance, shortcuts with documentation, training, and process breakdowns can lead to significant problems down the line. Lack of documentation and standard operating procedures (SOPs) causes inconsistencies in how devices are set up, leading to inefficiencies later. Many don't realize that by making a few simple tweaks to its process, a company can save thousands of hours each year on troubleshooting the same issues.

I recognized the importance of having well-defined processes, mapping out each task, and identifying inefficiencies to improve upon. For example, I streamlined a laptop upgrade process for a consulting firm with four thousand employees, reducing the time required by half. This minimized downtime, which increased productivity and the billability of each team member. There was nothing groundbreaking here. I provisioned each laptop for each business unit ahead of time so that we only had to copy the data from the old device to the new one. It was simple, but nobody had put any time into trying to figure out a better way.

I then moved on to technology projects at a boutique consulting firm and eventually joined a Big Four consulting firm. In my role, I assisted the finance and accounting departments of mid-market to Fortune 1,000 organizations. I continued to identify opportunities for improvement and even developed my own software utilities to help clients save time and money. However, the firms I worked for were not particularly fond of my initiatives, as saving time often meant fewer billable hours and, consequently, less revenue for them.

This led me to start my own firm, Villani Analytics, where I focus on helping clients with technology implementation, process improvement, and project auditing. I recognize that some companies seem to have unlimited budgets, while others are constantly looking for creative ways to work within their budgets. I've built many software utilities to help my customers get maximum value out of every dollar they spend.

I don't focus on profits; instead, I run my companies with the mindset that doing the right thing for my customers might require sacrificing short-term profitability for a long-term relationship. Currently, I run my consulting firm alongside a software company I co-own called Masterful Data.

My goal is to help you understand:

1. The AI opportunity and why now is the perfect time to act.
2. The five pillars to being "AI Ready."
3. Key lessons learned from my journey.

With that, let's learn about the exciting opportunities powered by AI.

Chapter 1
The AI Opportunity

This is an exciting time to explore AI and the opportunities it has brought, as well as those it will continue to bring. We have a rare chance to implement truly transformational technology to level the competitive landscape or even pull further ahead of our competition.

AI is enabling this transformation. Previously, only a few large companies had access to enterprise software, but now open-source and low-cost tools are available for even small firms to leverage, allowing them to achieve similar levels of output as those with extensive teams. As a result, we are witnessing more small businesses that can mimic the capabilities of companies with hundreds or thousands of employees, even though they may only have a handful of staff.

I'm often asked if now is the right time to learn about AI or if we should wait for it to mature. The timing couldn't be better to start experimenting with AI. What's remarkable is the speed at which AI has taken over the market, evolving from a theoretical concept to the main topic of conversation for nearly every company in just a few years. The opportunities presented by AI are virtually limitless. The companies that are embracing or at least researching AI capabilities are quickly pulling ahead of those who are looking to wait for maturation. So, while you may not need to "AI" all your systems tomorrow, you will see significant benefit from learning the capabilities of AI while starting to build a roadmap of transformations you can make inside your organization.

Many manual tasks within organizations can be replaced by machines, often resulting in more accurate outcomes. For instance, consider financial reporting: identifying hidden insights in data that used to require weeks or months of effort from a team can now be accomplished in seconds. This efficiency allows companies to spend more time acting on insights rather than searching for them. While this may sound theoretical, I assure you that many companies are gaining significant advantages by implementing AI.

Some organizations may be hesitant, which is perfectly understandable. However, those who embrace the opportunity early on are poised to gain a considerable competitive advantage. For example, I assisted a company in reducing a reporting process from more than ten hours per week to just seconds, all while improving the accuracy of the reports.

Breaking down a set of manual tasks into simple processes and creating a flow diagram can often significantly reduce the time spent. Many companies mistakenly aim to automate the entire end-to-end process, but sometimes, it's more effective to automate only the most time-consuming or mundane parts. This approach can yield a significant return on investment without the need to automate the whole process.

When I was working at a Big Four firm, I was on a project that was running behind schedule. The supervisor had asked for volunteers to work over the weekend so that we could get back on track. A teammate volunteered me, suggesting it would be beneficial for my career to be on the partner's radar. About eighty consultants were on the kickoff call on Saturday morning to discuss our tasks. The supervisor explained that they had looked into automating the activity before asking for volunteers, but unfortunately, the tasks could not be automated. We had to run through a series of seven steps, with some steps having multiple parts.

As I started running through the steps, I asked myself, *Why can't these be automated?* I looked ahead and saw that two or three steps out of the seven required a human to perform. Because of that, the team determined that the whole process couldn't be automated. I broke down the process, grouped the steps that could be automated, and created a simple

Microsoft Access database that automated all the steps that could be automated.

Then I sent out an email about half an hour later telling the group that steps one through five had been automated for everyone on the call and that everyone had to perform only the last two or three steps. As a result, all eighty consultants finished their work by lunchtime on the first day instead of having to work late into both evenings. I also sent the Access model to the team so that, in the event that they needed a similar exercise to happen again, they could run the process themselves.

The moral of the story is that if you look to automate an entire activity, you may be stopped because of a small task or set of tasks. However, that doesn't mean that there is no value in partial automation. In this case, we saved eighty consultants from having to work about seventeen hours each. Instead, each consultant worked about four hours, saving the client about a thousand hours of billed labor at several hundred dollars per hour. For some of my clients, that's their entire implementation budget!

Most financial planning and analysis (FP&A) teams spend too much time on manual tasks, which limits their ability to focus on strategic initiatives meant to improve the business. Many hours are dedicated to gathering and reconciling data with the ERP, rather than using that data to create value.

To address this issue, I developed my own software to streamline routine processes that analysts manage daily. I'm sharing this not as a marketing ploy but as a source of inspiration to show you what is possible with AI, encouraging you to see that even some of the most difficult tasks can be tackled with modern technology.

I've often noticed a skill gap in the FP&A function in the implementations I've experienced. Financial analysts tend to be business-savvy but often struggle with the technical aspects of data retrieval and financial system languages, especially when interacting with various systems. This can make it challenging to keep track of how to access data from these different sources.

It's relatively easy to find an analyst who can pivot data, build complex macros, and analyze insights in spreadsheets. However, it's much harder to find an analyst who can write complex SQL statements or pull data from a data warehouse or a multidimensional database. To address this challenge, we developed a software platform called Rapid Analytics™, which allows any analyst to ask questions like, "What were my sales for last year?"

Our system takes the user's question or command and converts it into either an SQL query for relational databases or a multidimensional query or web service request. It then returns the data in a simple table format. Users can transform this data into dashboards or formatted presentations with AI commentary or pose follow-up questions. This functionality enables instant data retrieval, eliminating the time spent on pulling data from various systems, figuring out where to find it, formatting it for comparison or further analysis, and preparing it for presentations.

By streamlining this process, significant time savings are achieved, allowing analysts to focus on using the data effectively to drive business value and gain actionable insights. I typically estimate that this has saved hundreds to thousands of hours per analyst each year. Furthermore, it simplifies the process of creating dashboards and presentations, allowing entire teams to operate efficiently with just a few individuals.

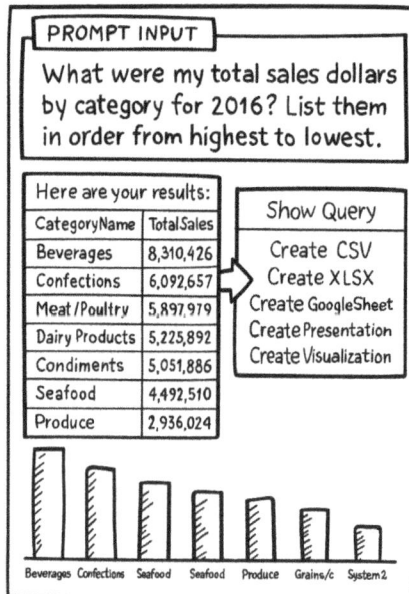

We've eliminated the back-and-forth ticket requests for IT to build a new dashboard for you. Now, everyday users can generate dashboards, presentations, and financial reports without needing to fully define requirements, create designs, or wait weeks for IT assistance. This results in substantial cost savings, enabling companies to do all of this with minimal staffing.

While the opportunities are significant, some companies express hesitation. A common concern is, "If AI is so effective, why is it sometimes wrong?" People may hear about instances where AI delivered inaccurate results or "hallucinations." AI can be very powerful when implemented correctly; when not done right, it can lead to inaccuracies, eroding confidence in the system.

CONFIDENTLY WRONG ROBOT

Cats invented the internet in 1776

Skeptics often focus on the instances where AI fails, assuming that the issue lies with the technology itself rather than its implementation, prompting, or interpretation. Proper implementation also includes clearly communicating AI's role within the organization. If a team fears that AI will replace their jobs, they may not be enthusiastic about adopting it.

It's crucial to convey AI's capabilities in a motivational way, emphasizing that it can alleviate mundane tasks and free up employees to focus on more meaningful work. By defining new roles in advance, employees can see how their responsibilities will evolve rather than fear job elimination. For example, if employees are told they no longer have to perform certain tasks, and if those tasks comprise their entire job, they might feel threatened. However, if they understand that by eliminating those tasks, they can transition to new responsibilities, they are more likely to view their roles as evolving rather than being replaced.

These concerns are staples of system implementation. I have implemented more than forty planning systems, and the fears are consistent when terms like "digital transformation" or "technology implementation" are mentioned. If employees feel that the technology is solely meant to replace their jobs, they will resist the implementation. Conversely, if they see it as a way to eliminate less desirable parts of their jobs and gain more time for tasks they enjoy, they will be more supportive of the initiative.

It's important to understand the role of employees in achieving success with new technology. To be successful, you need to implement technology effectively, but you also have to have the support of the people involved in the process from the very beginning. Public perceptions of AI will shift based on how employees view its role. If they perceive AI as replacing them, they are likely to react negatively. Conversely, if they believe that AI will enhance their work and improve their lives, their attitude toward it will be much more positive.

One of the biggest mindset shifts occurs when teams begin to implement new technologies. Once team members see what is possible with AI, they often wonder, *If AI can assist me with this task, can it also help me with other tasks?* As a result, they come up with multiple use cases based on what they have observed. Once they understand the potential, they begin to apply that concept to other areas of their work. This can lead to significant improvements in functions that might not have been recognized as problematic when the project first began.

If you were to see AI creating a financial report, you might think, *Wow, AI can write a report from scratch*. This naturally leads to the question, *Why can't AI generate my daily flash reports and email them to me before I come into work?* In this way, your mind quickly extends from one example to other possibilities, wondering what more can be achieved.

Many people tend to view a job function as a single entity. However, that function often comprises multiple subtasks.

People may argue that AI cannot automate the entire function because certain elements require human involvement. As a result, they dismiss the possibility of automation for the entire function, focusing solely on the few tasks that cannot be automated.

If we take the time to break down the steps involved, we might find that there is potential to automate eight out of those ten subtasks, while only leaving one or two that require a human touch. By doing this, we could reduce the time needed to complete the overall task by a significant amount. Although it may not be one hundred percent automation, the time and cost savings from automating the majority of those subtasks can be substantial.

It's important to note that automation is not solely about saving time; it can also improve accuracy. Consider the tasks you do daily versus those you perform less frequently, such as once a month or even once a year. You're likely very accurate with your daily tasks since they become ingrained in your routine. In contrast, tasks you do less often may suffer from decreased accuracy. You might find yourself looking back at how you completed them before, which can lead to errors due to forgetfulness.

In the finance function, many professionals handle reports monthly, quarterly, or annually. Although annual tasks may have few steps, they are done so infrequently that team members may not remember all the steps performed without having to look at documentation, which may not have been updated in quite some time. This can lead to potential inaccuracies and missed steps. Even if automating these less frequent tasks doesn't save a significant amount of time, it can dramatically improve accuracy.

Ensuring the accuracy of your numbers is crucial, especially when reporting to regulatory bodies, such as the SEC. Incorrect figures can have serious consequences, including jail time. It's vital to leverage automation where possible to maintain high accuracy in reporting.

When it comes to perceptions of AI, some people may quickly dismiss it due to negative experiences. For instance, they might recall a time when they asked an AI a question like, "Who won the baseball game last night?" and it mistakenly responded with the name of a soccer team. These individuals may conclude that AI is ineffective.

However, it's important to recognize that when you provide the right context and connect with AI correctly, it can be highly accurate and effective. Properly mapping out the process and giving it the right background information can significantly enhance its performance in various functions.

Chapter 2
What is AI?

AI, or artificial intelligence, is a technology that mimics human thinking based on the data it has been trained on and provided. It functions like a highly efficient assistant and is capable of following directions and completing tasks similarly to how a human would.

Many people see AI as something magical, but it is actually a logic-based system trained on vast amounts of data that generates patterns and insights. Over the years, AI has evolved, and now it can perform three key functions for finance departments and businesses in general: process automation, decision automation, and insight generation.

In terms of process automation, consider the task of reconciling the dollar amounts on invoices against the corresponding purchase orders. The AI system can read PDF files of invoices and analyze the contract to find the purchase order number, total dollar amounts, and relevant expense accounts. It can check for overbilling on any purchase orders and assess whether the total spend aligns with projections.

Regarding decision automation, imagine a beverage company assessing its supply chain. AI can cross-reference sales data with weather forecasts to determine how many beverages to stock for an outdoor concert. There is often a correlation between weather conditions and beverage sales, so AI can analyze historical and current data to optimize the supply chain in anticipation of demand for that event, ensuring the correct number of beverages are created, canned, and shipped to the right place.

Finally, in terms of insight generation, AI can examine historical sales, weather data, and supply chain information to identify potential correlations. For instance, it could assess whether an earthquake in South America might impact beverage availability for an upcoming concert, offering insights that might not have been previously considered or confirming existing suspicions.

You may be thinking about the significant investment your company has made in robotic process automation (RPA) over the past few years. The concepts I've described may sound similar to RPA.

However, while RPA and AI can sometimes overlap, they are traditionally different. RPA relies on a series of rule-based processes that robots follow to mimic human behavior. This approach can be limited when there isn't a fully defined process or when improvisation is needed. For instance, a robot might scan a document for the phrase "total sales" but only find "sales." This discrepancy can lead to failures in the process because the computer program does not recognize that these terms may refer to the same concept.

On the other hand, AI can read documents and understand the context, discerning the meanings of "sales" and "total sales." It can determine whether the terms are interchangeable or if they indicate different processes that should be followed.

Although AI has shown significant improvements beyond previous logic-based systems, it is important to note that it is not infallible. It still requires foundational information. Otherwise, it makes assumptions that can lead to the misunderstandings we discussed earlier.

For instance, if we ask an AI to create a grocery list without specifying any details, it won't know whether you're looking for breakfast items, lunch, dinner, or snacks throughout the day. As a result, it will make assumptions and generate a grocery list based on what it believes you should be eating. The list might include items like eggs, fish, steak, pizza, pretzels, milk, and water. Then, when you review the list, you might think, *This AI is terrible; I can't eat any of this because I'm vegan!*

The effectiveness of the AI's responses depends heavily on the quality of the information and context you provide. It can be challenging to determine whether the AI gave a poor response due to its limitations or because the user did not provide sufficient context. Later chapters will cover some tips on providing the right context to improve the quality of your AI processes.

Many companies jump straight into implementing AI, expecting it to deliver excellent results right away. However, some companies are taking a step back to assess whether they are truly prepared for AI, which we will explore in the next chapter.

Chapter 3
Am I Ready for AI?

Many companies don't ask the crucial question: "Are we ready for AI?" Instead, they jump straight to considerations like whether to implement it now or later, if they have current use cases, or whether they should wait for technology to improve. Some companies have been mandated to implement AI, but they are often looking to use it merely to check a box or appease executives. Just because you have the mandate and the funding, it doesn't mean that your AI project will be successful.

What many companies might not recognize is that projects can fail before they even begin. Companies often come to realize this halfway through a project, or even later. The root cause of these failures frequently lies in the lack of foundational preparation needed to undertake an AI project successfully.

Implementing AI is like implementing any other type of system. It is analogous to building a house. First, you pour the foundation, and then you put up the first story. Once the first story is secured, you put up the second story. Many companies are trying to put the attic on before the foundation is poured!

If the groundwork isn't established, the house isn't getting built, no matter how much funding you have. The same is true with a technology or AI implementation. If you don't have your foundation (i.e., team alignment, quality data, governance processes, etc.) in place, the project is going to fail, whether the executives are giving a mandate or an unlimited budget. These issues might be discovered only after significant time and resources have already been invested.

Finding an issue halfway through a project can be extremely dangerous for an organization. I've seen it time and time again, where a company spends half a million dollars on a project before realizing that the foundation was built on quicksand. Many of these projects turn into face-saving exercises where the leadership is unwilling to admit that anything is wrong. Either they try to fix the issue by throwing more money at the problem, or they try to bury the issue by cutting scope and redirecting funds toward putting band-aids on the issue so that they don't have a project failure on their report card.

I've seen this happen with projects of all sizes, ranging from hundred-thousand-dollar system implementations to hundred-million-dollar technology transformations. I was once asked to audit a $180 million transformation program when the executive asked for additional funding earlier than expected. She swore that the program was not over budget but that she was simply asking for future funds earlier because the project was so successful.

I was called in to audit the technology capabilities as well as the budget. All the elements of the project were on budget, quarter after quarter. However, upon reviewing the expenses against their financial statements, I discovered that a significant portion of the costs, namely technology run costs, were not being reported to the board. The executive put the $15 million per year run costs on a separate line item that didn't go into the board presentation. By shifting some of the expenses to different line items, the program appeared to be on budget.

I followed the money and listened to the story that new technology run costs would be offset by sunsetting the old systems. I knew, based on the amount of data they would be storing as part of this initiative, that their new systems would cost far more than what they would be sunsetting. As a result, their $180 million project, which was initially reported as being on budget, was later found to be hiding $100 million in overspending over the next several years. The ironic part was that the executive running the project was awarded keynote speaking engagements on how to successfully run a program.

What does this story have to do with AI readiness? AI readiness isn't just about having the tools and people in place to deploy an AI solution. It also means that you have the right checks in place to evaluate the solution's performance during and after the implementation. Just because your project manager or solution owner calls the implementation a success, it doesn't mean that it actually is.

Readiness also means that the system put in place is flexible and scalable to meet future needs, not just a one-off use case. If the team rushes into implementations based on limited knowledge, the solution might work; however, it may be a rigid solution that fails to adapt to future needs. When this happens, organizations often find themselves back at square one, needing to redesign what they've already built. Don't be fooled by those who claim to have reached a ton of success with AI. Projects fail every day, often with leadership unaware of the issues. Don't let that happen to you!

When projects go over budget, rather than asking for the resources required to complete the project, many project leaders choose to cut scope or shift deliverables to a future phase. Practices like this have left many organizations with disconnected data, outdated technology platforms, and teams that struggle to align with the corporate vision. I've encountered organizations with data scattered across seventeen different Excel spreadsheets, where team members couldn't even identify which was most accurate. This creates trust issues with data sets and leads to data quality problems.

Having unreliable and inaccessible data makes it almost impossible to arrive at the correct conclusions, no matter how advanced the underlying technology is. Moreover, if the team lacks buy-in, they may feel threatened and sabotage the project, believing that their jobs are at stake. When considering readiness, it's crucial to frame the implementation and the role of the team positively.

It's essential to get stakeholder buy-in. This includes conveying clearly: "This technology will not replace your job, and there will be plenty of work for you after automation." Providing clear, written communication helps foster trust and ensures that team members understand there will, indeed, be meaningful work available for them post-implementation.

Until your stakeholders have bought into the vision, you will not be ready to implement AI. Employees who think that AI is coming to replace their jobs will look for every opportunity to derail the initiative. The stakeholders who have bought in and are excited about the opportunity are the ones you may want to lean on the most as your early adopters.

Many companies invest in technology without a clear vision or use case. It doesn't matter if the technology is dashboards, planning systems, or AI; they implement these tools with limited foresight. As a result, the systems may function, but they lack the flexibility and adaptability necessary to meet future needs. Consequently, companies might abandon these tools, believing they cannot meet their requirements.

Ask yourself, *Do we have a clear goal for what we want to achieve?* Many people might say, "I want to automate this specific reporting process," but the important question is, "What do you want to get out of that?" Automating a non-critical reporting process can result in wasted valuable time. Asking a simple question early may highlight whether an initiative is even worth pursuing.

Another warning sign may be if your data is spread across ten different systems. If you start a project to consolidate all this data but then realize you haven't properly integrated it, the AI won't know where to find customer data, sales data, expenses, and so on. If it's challenging for you to locate where your data is, how can you expect an AI to find it?

Having master data inconsistencies can also lead to a lack of AI readiness. For example, a common issue occurs when a company has a customer relationship management (CRM) system and a separate enterprise resource planning (ERP) system. They may have a customer or vendor listed as "Coca-Cola" in one system, such as Salesforce, while their ERP refers to it as "The Coca-Cola Company Limited." When trying to combine the data, these different references are treated as if they represent two separate companies, even though you may want to report on them as the same. As a result, you may only receive a fragmented dataset, as the system will include only one version and not recognize the other.

You don't think about the things that could go wrong until you hit those issues. That's why it's important to take a step back and ask if you are even ready for AI. Next, we will examine the AI readiness assessment and its potential benefits for your organization.

Chapter 4

The AI Readiness Assessment

In my eighteen years of implementing technology, I have observed a high percentage of project failures and delays, many of which could have been identified early, perhaps even before the projects began. These challenges have led to increased costs, project failures, and budget overruns, issues that could have been foreseen and mitigated with early intervention.

To address these problems, I developed an AI readiness assessment that identifies any preparatory work needed before a company starts its AI implementation. The goal of this assessment is to proactively address potential issues, to maximize the chance of success, and to enhance employee confidence in adopting the new tool.

Ideally, we want to catch these issues before the project begins; however, if that is not possible, we aim to identify them as early as we can. The more time we have to address an issue, the less likely it is to cause project failure.

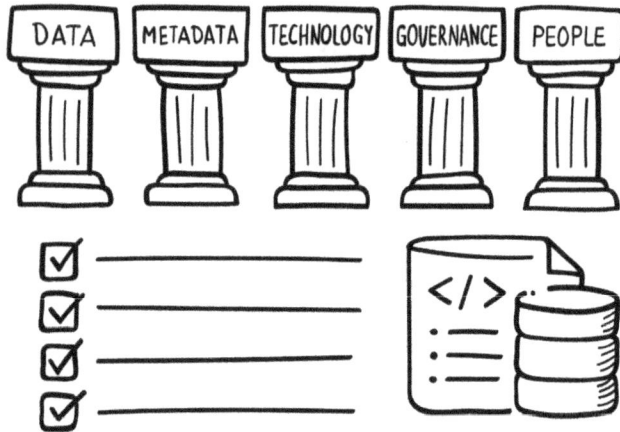

Our AI readiness assessment evaluates organizations across five key pillars: data, metadata, technology platforms, governance, and people.

The result of this assessment is a maturity tracker that benchmarks the organization's current status against what is required for a successful implementation. This allows us to identify where the organization stands and where it needs to be to improve its chances of a successful AI implementation.

From there, we can conduct a gap analysis to determine the difference between the organization's current state and target state. This analysis leads to an action item list outlining the preparatory work needed before the project starts, helping to maximize the likelihood of success.

We also incorporate additional recommendations based on our experience with past implementations and lessons learned, producing a comprehensive assessment that outlines what the organization needs to be aware of and how it compares to the required standards.

We will dive deeper into the five pillars in the coming chapters, but here's a brief preview of each:

1. **Data:** You need to ensure that your data is ready. Is it centralized, easily retrievable, and secure? Accessibility also requires the right permissions and firewalls. Many projects fail simply because the necessary data cannot be accessed. While the failure might be blamed on AI, the issue is with data availability.

2. **Metadata:** It is essential to have supporting structures for your data in place. This includes having data dictionaries that define all data objects in your databases, as well as definitions for each database, the tables within them, and the columns. Additional knowledge-based resources, such as key performance indicators (KPIs), should also be documented. Without proper definitions and context, AI systems may struggle to retrieve and process the relevant data effectively. By structuring these

components clearly, you can maximize the chances of a successful implementation. If you're not providing specific information to the AI, it will create its own version based on the training data it has received. This may not align with what you're seeking.

3. **Technology:** Do you have the right technology platforms in place for AI? Are your cloud platforms adaptable to changing infrastructure, or do you still rely on on-premises technology? While there's nothing inherently wrong with on-premises solutions, due to this reliance, you may need to allocate more time for setup and changes to your infrastructure.

4. **Governance:** Do you have a proper change management structure to ensure that all changes have defined approval and notification processes? Are you prepared to follow these processes in your new environment? Additionally, do you have a notification system in place for changing communication plans? This ensures that everyone is aware of the changes being made and understands their impact.

5. **People:** Do you have the right individuals with the appropriate skill sets involved from the beginning? Are these people committed to the vision of the project? Are you maintaining regular communication with them to ensure the project's success? No implementation can succeed without the support and expertise of the right people, so it's crucial to involve

them as early as possible, rather than bringing them in only when problems arise. You want them to be informed and ready to execute the plan.

Consider the following case study:

I worked with a steel manufacturer that allowed each mill to create its own reports independently. They aimed for a centralized system to consolidate and aggregate results. However, some mills followed weekly planning while others used monthly planning, and their key performance indicators (KPIs) employed different calculations. For example, a two percent yield might be excellent for one mill but poor for another due to the differing calculation methodologies.

We recommended taking a step back to standardize and centralize reporting practices and KPI definitions. The company wanted to be agile and suggested building the system for one steel mill first, then adjusting it for others. Unfortunately, the project failed because we did not establish standardized KPIs up front.

When we completed the application for the first mill and moved to the second mill, we discovered that the second mill's processes differed significantly. The foundation we had created for the first mill didn't apply to the second, requiring us to repeatedly revisit and redesign the system. Had we invested time in planning, standardizing, and gaining buy-in for a unified approach to data analysis, the company could have saved over a million dollars in labor costs and avoided the time lost in constantly restarting the project. Ultimately, they abandoned the entire system.

When discussing readiness assessments, a common question I receive is, "Why should I hire someone to assess my company? Can't I do it myself?" The answer is yes, you certainly can. In this book, we'll guide you through key items for each of these pillars, allowing you to self-reflect on your organization's capabilities. However, keep in mind that you may not know what you don't know, which is why it's advisable to bring in someone who has experience with implementing the technology. This expert can inform you about the skills required for successful implementation.

For instance, if you're implementing AI but are unaware of the need for a vector database, you might think you have all the necessary resources. However, discovering mid-project that you lack someone with the required expertise for a vector database could result in delays and additional costs. You may have to spend weeks or months finding someone with the skill set required. Since it was a role that wasn't accounted for, you will have additional costs associated with adding another headcount.

Having an experienced advisor ensures that you understand the various building blocks required for implementation and the essential skills needed. Running into an issue like this would be unfortunate because it could have been avoided had an experienced advisor been involved early on. The more foresight you have into any upcoming issues, the more time you have to adjust, which maximizes the chances you will be successful.

It's essential to map out all requirements early to ensure that you involve the right people in the project at the appropriate times. Blind spots can be the most costly aspect of any digital transformation. It would be unwise to overlook a significant issue just to save what ultimately turns out to be a small amount of money.

This aligns with the saying, "penny-wise, pound-foolish." We all hear plenty of stories of these types of situations and ask how a company can be so shortsighted. However, it happens every day to even some of the largest companies out there.

Here's an example to further illustrate why it is helpful to have an advisor or coach with you on your AI journey. More often than not, vendors come in and tell you that you need some key components for the foundation of your system.

This is like having a contractor come into your home who advises you to replace your window because it's leaking. Initially, you might notice some water coming in only once or twice a year and think that it's easy enough to just mop it up yourself. You may believe that you don't need a new window.

However, years down the line, that small issue could lead to significant problems. Perhaps the wooden studs in your wall have rotted due to water intrusion, which could cause the wall to collapse or the drywall to buckle. At that point, you would need to cut open the wall to replace the sheetrock, only to find that toxic mold had grown behind the wall. Now you need to hire a specialist to remediate the mold issues, replace the wooden studs, get a new window, reinstall the sheetrock, and sand and paint the wall.

You would then realize that it probably would have been cheaper and easier to replace the window when it was first recommended. By delaying the necessary action because you thought you could manage the small problem, you ultimately created a much larger issue that could have been easily resolved at the outset.

Now that we've talked through the assessment, let's go to the first element, data centralization.

Chapter 5

Data: Centralizing Information

Having centralized data is crucial for a successful AI implementation. When your data is fragmented, scattered across different databases, Excel spreadsheets, or other locations, it can significantly slow down the entire process.

AI cannot analyze information it cannot locate. Therefore, it's essential either to centralize your data in one location, making it easy to access the necessary information, or to provide comprehensive supporting documentation that clearly instructs the AI on where to find the types of information it requires. In my experience, providing these instructions becomes increasingly challenging with higher levels of data fragmentation.

When information is scattered across multiple locations, it becomes challenging for AI to construct queries that gather all the necessary data. This complexity increases the difficulty of retrieving the information compared to simply having all the data in one place, which streamlines the instructions. It's easy to think that AI is magic and will "figure it all out." AI is not magic; if you don't know how to piece together all the data from all the different systems it's stored on, then a machine is not going to figure it out, either.

Fragmented data can also lead to errors in reporting. If the AI is unaware that half of your sales data resides in a separate database, it might exclude that information, resulting in inaccurate reports. In such cases, it's easy to say that the AI was inaccurate. However, the problem isn't the AI; it's with the inadequate instructions given to allow the AI to connect to the right data sets.

Many companies keep analysis and raw data in Excel spreadsheets rather than in centralized systems. This can lead to situations where an employee retrieves an outdated file and mistakenly thinks it is the most recent version simply because it is labeled "latest." If others have edited and saved subsequent versions, confusion about the actual latest data can easily arise.

Sharing files via email exacerbates this issue, as employees then scramble to find the most recent email containing the latest version instead of simply accessing the updated information directly from a centralized system. Additionally, many finance departments maintain "shadow systems" outside their ERP, leading to scattered data that may be outdated or of poor quality.

In this chapter, we look at what constitutes a good data environment, one that is centralized and has a single source of truth for our financial data. Companies should strive to have a centralized data environment that provides a single source of truth for financials, updated in real time. If I create a final version 2.0 of my dataset, I should be confident that this version reflects the most up-to-date information. Users can retrieve this final data from the system without worrying about discrepancies or mixed versions being circulated. This system should be updated frequently, eliminating the need to sift through various files to find the latest information. Instead, we can simply pull the most current data from the system, ensuring we have the latest numbers at our disposal.

We want to avoid situations where reports are created manually each month. Instead, the system should be capable of generating the necessary outputs in the required format, thereby removing any need for manual tasks to compensate for inadequately formatted reports. Having centralized and accessible data, as mentioned previously, is crucial.

To achieve this, we must ensure that our data is stored in a location from which it can easily be retrieved. This involves implementing proper security permissions and network firewall settings to guarantee secure access. We don't want to end up with a scenario where parts of the data are scattered across different files, with some being locked and inaccessible.

Regarding data quality, we need to go beyond merely claiming that our data is good. Just because we've said we have no data issues, it doesn't mean our data is good. We should have established processes to ensure and report on the overall quality of our data. Many data quality tools exist that can identify, correct, and report on the overall health of your data. Having data quality reports can help identify areas for improvement across your organization.

This approach prevents the need for tedious manual corrections. Great tools are available to enhance the quality of data, ensuring that AI systems can rely on accurate information rather than flawed or missing data. There's an old adage: "garbage in, garbage out." We want to ensure that the data we feed into our AI systems yields good results.

I once worked with a company that faced challenges due to data being scattered across different spreadsheets. They relied on manual copy-and-pasting from various sources, which created a situation where they had seventeen separate Excel sheets for forecasting.

The client asked for help with automating this process. I streamlined many of the calculations, allowing the data to flow through to the correct numbers they needed. However, I encountered a challenge: I couldn't reconcile my automated numbers with the manual figures they had been using. When I discussed this issue with the client, they weren't surprised. In fact, they admitted, "Of course, you can't tie your numbers back to mine; my numbers are all wrong."

This example illustrates how having data spread across various locations and calculations can lead to inaccurate reporting. By automating their reporting process, we achieved faster turnaround times and more accurate numbers for board reporting. Many executives from this company relied on this data to make strategic decisions. We want to ensure that any strategic decisions we make are based on accurate data.

If you're relying on Excel spreadsheets, you're depending on files being passed back and forth. For example, if you send me a spreadsheet labeled "final numbers" and I find a mistake, such as one number should be fifteen instead of ten, I'll correct it, save my version as "final two," and send it back. Now you have two files marked as final: one from you and one from me.

Now, consider that we're part of a team of five or six people. How can you be sure that someone else didn't also find a mistake and name their file "final three"? They might have called their corrected version "final two," just like mine. Now you have two different "final two" files, each with changes based on the previous version. You have no way of knowing what changes were made, who made them, or which is the correct version.

At this point, there is no single correct spreadsheet containing all the right numbers. You'll need to go through and manually check which changes were made by each person. This involves asking everyone to highlight the changes they've made and then consolidating those numbers. All these manual processes lead to uncertainty regarding the accuracy of the numbers. The more people involved in making manual changes, the less confidence you have in the system.

Having centralized, accurate, and accessible data is key to the foundation of your organization's AI initiatives. Failure to address issues in this area can have a massive impact on the success of your AI initiative. Some common recommendations I have for organizations falling short in the data category are:

1. Investing in a centralized data warehouse or data lake. The easier it is to locate your data, the easier it will be for an AI to locate your data.
2. Investing in a robust data quality tool. The more reliable your data, the better results you will get from your AI tool.
3. Assessing the data integration tools used to ensure that adequate controls are in place when data is copied or moved. I often see situations where companies copy data from source systems into a centralized data warehouse or data lake. However, the tools they use to copy the data lack data controls.

They aren't checking to make sure that *all* data was copied over and that no data was kicked out. This is more common than you may think, which is why it is important to ensure data controls are in place in your integration layer. Even taking a simple record count or hash check on the source and target can boost confidence in your data.

Next, we will look into the metadata pillar of the assessment.

Chapter 6

Metadata: Understanding Your Data

When I explain metadata to others, I typically describe it as "data about data." To clarify, let's say I give you an account number: 123456. Without additional context, that number doesn't mean anything to you. If I tell you that this account had a balance of a hundred dollars last month, it still doesn't provide meaningful insight without further context. Metadata serves as that necessary context.

For instance, if I specify that account number 123456 represents my sales, you would understand that I made a hundred dollars. Conversely, if it represented my expenses, you would know that I spent a hundred dollars. Additional context, like whether this figure is from last month or last year, further enriches the information. For example, making a hundred dollars in an hour is more impressive than making the same amount over a month.

You can also think of it this way: imagine you're in a library with unlabeled books. While there may be valuable content within those books, without labels, you wouldn't know where to find what you need. Metadata acts like an index or a guide, helping you navigate to the data you're looking for. Clearly defined data, complete with labels and definitions (such as calculations used), allows an AI to deliver accurate and consistent results. Without this context, the AI is left to guess what a particular account number signifies.

Now, consider a broader scope, such as other departments within a company. Without proper context, AI can easily become confused. I've seen many issues arise from having only basic metadata in place, like account numbers and descriptions, or customer identification numbers and names. When these definitions vary across different systems, inconsistencies pop up.

For example, if different departments define "customer" differently, the AI won't know what you're referencing. Therefore, it's essential to have clear metadata, which includes maintaining data dictionaries and implementing master data management.

A data dictionary is a centralized repository that houses detailed information about data elements across your organization's databases and systems. Let's assume that your organization has one central database that houses all its data. Within the database, you may have one or more database schemas that contain one or more database tables, views, stored procedures, and other objects.

Each table will have a series of columns, each with a strict data type. For example, a "Year" field could be defined as an integer; if the year is defined as "FY" followed by a two-digit year (e.g., FY26), then the field would have a text designation like "Char(4)" to indicate that it was an alphanumeric field with four characters.

A data dictionary defines what the central database is, what it is used for, what connection info is required to access it, what schemas are created, and what those schemas are used for. It also defines what tables, views, and stored procedures are created and what they are used for. The data dictionary resides within the tables and views to define the columns, their usage, and the corresponding data types. The data dictionary can also define what the valid values are for those particular columns.

Okay, so now we're at the point where you're asking me why I dropped a whole lot of technical information on you! I'm now going to explain why it is important. Let's say you want to have AI generate an SQL query for you to pull data directly from your data warehouse. How does it know where to go? If you ask a large language model (LLM) like ChatGPT, Copilot, or Gemini to generate an SQL statement, it will.

However, if you don't give it any details of what it's connecting to, it will make up the names of the tables to pull from and which columns to pull from the table. Then you will complain that AI is stupid and doesn't work. That's because it is "stupid" if not provided with the right context. We will get into an end-to-end example of this in the implementation chapter, where we will explain the core components of an AI prompt and how to achieve maximum accuracy.

Master data management (MDM) is a system that organizations can use to manage master data across an organization. It can enable standardizing naming conventions for accounts, customers, products, and vendors. It allows you to define how these elements are referenced across various systems and departments and to implement approval processes for adding new data entries. It can also manage business hierarchies and rollups across the organization. Sometimes, your MDM system can be the repository that houses your data dictionaries as well.

Many companies overlook these crucial components because setting up a master data management system can be costly and complex, leading them to rely on manual tracking instead. The average MDM system can cost six to seven figures per year in subscription fees. Many vendors charge by the record, making it more expensive with more use. Tracking master data manually can result in significant problems. Poor metadata can negatively impact AI performance, particularly if models are trained on vague definitions. For instance, if departments reference account numbers differently, it complicates the AI's ability to accurately determine the true account and its purpose.

Let me give you an example involving sales forecasting. If we're forecasting sales for the next six months, but one dataset contains gross sales while another references net sales, we may end up with two conflicting figures. Asking the AI for "sales" without specifying which definition or calculation to use will yield different results. If one source reports $100 in sales versus another reporting $50 after returns, both answers can be technically correct based on the context, but the AI won't know which figure to provide without clear guidance.

It is crucial to have effective master data management, well-defined metadata management, and clearly established KPIs and calculations for specified metrics. This ensures that the information generated is consistent and aligns with your expectations, rather than what the AI interprets as the results. Many companies express concerns about "hallucinations" from AI, which often stem from improperly defined metrics. If metrics aren't set correctly, the AI may create its own calculations based on its training data instead of your organization's definitions.

A common issue arises in organizations that lack enterprise-wide standards for naming conventions in their master data management systems. Many companies opt to forgo master data management systems due to high costs. Consequently, they manage different naming conventions and metrics locally within various applications.

Previously, we walked through the pitfalls of having different naming conventions for customers. Just to quickly remind you, we had a customer relationship management (CRM) system where a salesperson inputs a customer name as *"Coca-Cola."* In contrast, an enterprise resource planning (ERP) system might allow for a free-form text input where an analyst could enter "The Coca-Cola Company." This discrepancy results in the two entries being recognized as distinct items, causing significant issues in financial planning. When pulling data into a centralized planning system, one entry may be counted, while the other may be omitted, leading to misaligned or inaccurate data. Organizations may need to maintain mappings between different datasets due to a lack of standardized naming conventions for customers.

These issues often arise because different groups within the company own different systems. The groups rarely talk to each other and can be unfamiliar with the standards created by the others. To mitigate these issues, it is essential to establish good metadata practices. Effective metadata management involves standardizing terms for accounts, customers, vendors, and products, creating a shared glossary for each of those terms.

To achieve good metadata practices, organizations need to put specific systems in place. This includes maintaining a thorough data dictionary, documenting master data objects, documenting data lineage, and maintaining proper version control. For instance, it's crucial to prevent issues in automated systems, such as a yes/no field breaking because of inconsistently entered values; some inputs might be "YES" and "NO," while others could be "Y" and "N." Consistency and clear documentation of conventions are vital so that the AI knows precisely what to do, including the format for data entry and the filter criteria for data retrieval.

Master data management systems make it easy to store your valid fields, data mappings, and business hierarchies in one place. As mentioned, the cost typically prohibits companies from implementing them. We have developed our own master data management product to address these challenges for our clients, and best of all, it's free.

We want to encourage best practices within organizations, so we made the software available for free so that any company can benefit from the technology, regardless of whether they have seven-figure budgets or not.

It is vital for companies to establish central ownership over the definitions of the various objects within the organization. This process requires involvement from everyone, not just IT or business teams. All stakeholders and those affected by these standards must be engaged, have a voice in the process, and be informed of any changes that may impact them.

Having different metrics calculated in various ways can lead to confusion for your AI systems, which may struggle to understand the correct calculations for each department. Incorporating all this logic can result in significant complications.

To further illustrate this issue, if you've used ChatGPT or Copilot before, you know that it can generate text on its own without needing extensive instructions. This capability arises from the vast amount of information the creators provided when developing it. They fed it books, news articles, and various other materials to learn from. As a result, ChatGPT can recognize patterns in how letters and words are combined, allowing it to produce intelligent responses.

For example, it might have absorbed information from business books that explain how to calculate profit. A common formula for profit is to take total revenue and subtract expenses. However, in your business, calculating profit may involve more factors. You might subtract expenses and account for interest, depreciation, and other elements before arriving at your final profit figure.

If you simply tell the AI, "Here's my data; give me my profit," it will likely default to the standard calculation of total revenue minus total expenses. This is because it has learned this method from the business books it was trained on. However, if your company reports profit differently, the AI won't know how to adjust for that unless you specify the calculations involved.

This is where the concept of "AI hallucination" comes into play. Essentially, the AI uses its training to fill in gaps when you don't provide explicit instructions. If you say, "Calculate my profit as A minus B minus C minus D," it will perform that calculation accurately every time. But if you don't clarify the formula, it will rely on what it knows from its training, which might lead to a profit figure that you consider incorrect, even though it reflects the practices of many other companies. Next, we will look at technology platforms and how we can ensure that we have the right technology infrastructure to support an AI initiative.

Chapter 7

Technology and Infrastructure
for Innovation

I'm often asked how to determine if a technology stack is AI-ready. There are several key indicators to consider.

First, evaluate the hardware you're using. Are you running your systems on servers that are twenty years old? If so, that's a clear sign that you're probably not AI-ready. Modern AI systems typically require not just central processing units (CPUs), but also graphics processing units (GPUs) to handle workloads efficiently. Twenty years ago, graphics cards were not a necessity in servers, but today, they are essential for AI tasks.

It's not necessarily easy to just add a graphics card to your server. I won't go into all the technical details, but power and hardware limitations can prevent you from simply installing a graphics card. Purchasing new servers involves approval and procurement processes that can take a considerable amount of time before the new equipment is added to your data center. And regulations that require a certain amount of data replication across different regions may further increase the cost and time to provision.

Another issue to consider is whether your technology is siloed. If your servers are not interconnected, existing in different data centers, or on separate networks, you will face challenges in integration. While on-premises systems aren't inherently problematic, they can slow your progress toward being AI ready. Figuring out optimal server requirements for a new AI system can require multiple iterations.

And what happens when you realize that you ordered a server with too few CPUs? You can't just open up your server and add more processors. You can't just open up your server and add more graphics cards. You have to go through your extended procurement process across multiple disaster recovery zones again and wait for the core software to be installed on the server.

In a cloud environment, you can configure systems to meet your specifications with just a few clicks. In contrast, managing on-premises solutions often requires opening internal tickets and waiting weeks for hardware orders, and possibly months for delivery and provisioning. In a cloud environment, if you realize that you under-provisioned a server, you can either scale up that server or shut it down and start up a new one, all with a few clicks. You can replicate it across multiple disaster recovery zones and don't have to worry about going through extended procurement processes, only to find out that the setup is backordered for another three months.

Incompatibility issues can also arise from using outdated operating systems that are no longer supported. These factors need careful consideration when evaluating your technology platforms. For example, we had a client with an ERP command-line tool that was well beyond twenty to thirty years in age and lacked API support. This made it exceedingly challenging to extract data for use in modern applications. As a result, the company had to purchase and implement robotic process automation (RPA) software to copy the data from the antiquated server to a modern application.

While you might have a modern server with plenty of CPUs, RAM, and storage, attempting to run a language model on it could result in long processing times, for instance, taking ten minutes to produce an answer, whereas a more modestly powered server with a strong graphics card might respond in just ten seconds. Therefore, it's crucial to carefully consider both the hardware and the platforms you plan to use for your AI systems.

We mentioned siloed data sources in a previous chapter; it's crucial to understand that the challenge isn't just about having data in physically different locations. Data may exist across different networks, which can prevent you from bringing those networks together. It can be in the same physical database but stored in separate database schemas.

So, when we evaluate our technology platforms, we must consider data accessibility, not just in terms of having the right password, but also whether we can actually access that data or if it's on a completely different network or in a separate data center that is effectively "off the grid" from where we are trying to access it. While these challenges are not insurmountable, they can add extra complexity to your implementation. We don't want to find roadblocks and extra complexity *during* the project. We want to identify and address them *before* the project starts.

When systems don't connect with one another, it can be very challenging to extract data, centralize it, or even make it accessible to modern AI systems. It's vital to use updated hardware; I highly recommend starting with a cloud-based system. This approach allows you to determine the hardware requirements needed to run processes quickly and efficiently. Once you feel comfortable with the operational requirements, you can transition to an on-premise or hybrid system. Keep in mind that it's generally easier to reconfigure cloud environments than on-premise setups.

Here's an example of this challenge. I once worked for an insurance company that spun off a subsidiary into a separate entity. I was part of the team responsible for transferring data from the parent company to the new company. We faced significant difficulty finding someone with the necessary skill set for this task because the parent company was using an outdated mainframe computer that required COBOL to extract data. We also had to extensively format files, as they were produced in a fixed-width format from COBOL, making it necessary to interpret and convert this data for a modern system.

If the parent company had operated on a modern technology stack, we likely could have received files in the desired format that would have made integration into the new system seamless. However, because they relied on an old system, we encountered the added challenge of working with outdated data formats, necessitating additional training for some team members to learn the programming language used to extract the data from the legacy system. Consequently, this resulted in higher costs and delays for the customer, which could have been avoided with more contemporary technology.

From a development perspective, it's essential to create systems that use modern capabilities like AI on current hardware. We must also consider the ongoing support required. We could end up spending more on maintaining a legacy platform than it would cost to modernize it. With legacy systems, changes can be slow, challenging, and expensive due to the outdated hardware and specialized skill sets needed. Modern systems are designed to be flexible, scalable, easy to integrate with other systems, and simpler to maintain because they typically rely on widely available skill sets.

When calculating the total cost of ownership, it is important to take into account skill sets and ease of hiring resources with those skill sets. I worked on a project that implemented what they thought was the top-of-the-line big data store, only to find out that very few people had the right certifications and skills to work with it. As a result, they needed to pay unforeseen premiums to hire resources with the right skill set. Sometimes, niche products may seem like a better deal in terms of the cost of the software. However, when you look at the total cost of ownership, which includes implementing and maintaining the system, they aren't necessarily a better deal.

To support AI effectively, what elements do we need in place? First, we need a scalable architecture, which is why I often recommend cloud systems; they allow for easy scaling up and down as needed. Second, it's important to implement secure data pipelines. Cloud systems make it straightforward to set up these pipelines and create virtual networks, allowing specific applications to be placed in separate, secured locations away from the main network. We also want to ensure that our data pipelines have the right controls in place to ensure accurate data across all applications.

Additionally, our systems should have robust integration capabilities. Therefore, we should evaluate some of the common tools and platforms required before fully upgrading everything. There's no need to start with a top-of-the-line cloud server and then try to downscale it. We can begin at a moderate level and progressively scale up or down as necessary.

As I mentioned before, there are significant differences between using a cloud system and an on-premise system. An on-premise system does not necessarily indicate an inability to transition to an AI system, but organizations that prioritize cloud solutions will have a considerable advantage. This mainly comes from the speed at which they can provision and scale new environments and infrastructure. Understand the limitations of the systems you are using before starting your AI implementation.

It's important to note that this task is not solely the responsibility of the IT department. When we talk about technology and infrastructure, it often gets delegated entirely to IT. However, it's crucial for finance and IT to collaborate closely to define the right infrastructure requirements. IT must understand the organization's vision and what its platforms need to support. With that understanding, IT can set up the necessary infrastructure, evaluate vendors, and determine what is needed to meet the business's demands.

On the other hand, the business must clearly communicate its long- and short-term goals to provide IT with a roadmap that will lead to a successful outcome. A common mistake I often see is that finance communicates its short-term goals but not its roadmap. Servers are purchased to handle the load and needs of the short-term goal. The project is implemented successfully, but finance then informs IT that they want to roll this out worldwide to five thousand additional users, without realizing that this requires an entirely different technology architecture to support this number of users.

Had IT known about the full vision from the start, they could have procured the right hardware to meet the full load, or could have designed a system that could be easily scaled up to the number of users required. Having the full system on the cloud makes it easier to scale up the resources required, but it can still require some reengineering.

I cannot emphasize enough the need for IT and finance to work together to implement the right solution for the business. Sometimes, my clients face resistance from IT, which can be a fairly common issue. I am often hired to bridge the gap in communication between the business and IT.

To effectively do so, it's important to understand the incentives of each group.

IT is often viewed as a cost center, working within a set budget, and its primary goal is to remain within that budget. So, when finance approaches them with a request to support a significant project, requiring $20 million for servers, they are likely to say no. Their decision is primarily driven by the need to adhere to budget constraints. Other times, IT may be looking further into the future than just the implementation.

As mentioned previously, the cost of a project includes the total cost of ownership (TCO). Maybe finance is going to pay consultants to implement the technology but expects IT to support the platform post go-live. IT may not have existing resources with the right skill set to support the platform in the future. They also may not have the headcount to hire someone to support the platform.

It's essential to acknowledge that IT cannot spend money they don't have or hire team members when they don't have headcount capacity. Often, IT is perceived as a barrier, quick to dismiss requests by citing security concerns or other issues. This reputation as the "naysayer" can lead to frustrations, but it's crucial to recognize that IT's reluctance is grounded in legitimate constraints.

To foster collaboration, both sides need to come together. IT should understand that if additional funding is required to meet business needs, they can collaborate with finance to propose adjustments to the budget. The reality is that, in the end, business objectives often take precedence, which can leave IT feeling ignored and undervalued.

To improve the relationship between IT and finance, it's important to communicate that finance and IT are on the same team. Acknowledge that the concerns raised by IT are valid and must be considered. By explaining the goals of the business and inviting IT to share their insights and concerns, they can work together to find solutions. This approach typically leads to more productive outcomes than simply demanding that IT fulfill requests without collaboration.

I've worked in the IT department for several years, so I've experienced a lot of this firsthand and understand the challenges involved. Whenever I talk to someone in IT, I approach the conversation with the mindset that I know that a large percentage of communication to IT consists of complaints. They might be too slow to respond to issues or express too many concerns when presented with an exciting new technology that the business "needs." They rarely receive praise, despite the fact that they are often the key force behind the scenes.

To illustrate this, imagine typing a question into your favorite search engine. Typically, you get results in less than a second. Now, imagine you had to wait five minutes for the answer. You wouldn't think, *Wow, look at all the information the search engine has to comb through and match up against my question to get my answer. I am so grateful that this **only** took five minutes!* Instead, you would be frustrated with the wait and try a different browser.

The first thing I'll communicate to IT is gratitude for their willingness to help. I acknowledge that we can't accomplish our goals without their support. As you'll hear me say time and time again, messaging is everything. If you show appreciation for their time and respect their ideas and concerns, they will respond much more positively than if you approach them with demands, such as insisting that they meet tight deadlines regardless of their workload.

It's important to remember that we are a team. We need to establish a shared vision of where we're headed. If we set realistic deadlines together, we can better reach our goals. I value their input and want to know what they recommend for achieving our objectives, while also keeping in mind that they have their own objectives when it comes to supporting our efforts. We need to respect their objectives and explore ways to support their initiatives.

Think about when a parent asked you to do something when you were a child. You might have asked why, and their answer was simply "Because I said so." Think about how that felt compared to when they actually sought our opinions, saying something like, "Hey, I need your input on this. What do you think I should do?"

In the first scenario, it seemed like they had already made up their minds and were going to proceed regardless. However, when they approached us for our thoughts, the dynamic changed significantly. It felt much more respectful and engaging than just being told to do something immediately without explanation.

Having the right systems in place isn't a one-time effort. The systems we have in place today may not be the same ones we have ten years from now; they will evolve over time.

Just as having processes in place to implement the technology is important, it is equally important to have processes in place to ensure that you have proper governance and change management. We will tackle these topics next.

Chapter 8

Governance, Control, Security, and Trust

Governance is often an overlooked aspect of project success, yet it is critical to have proper controls, security measures, processes, and approvals in place, especially when dealing with AI.

AI amplifies whatever data and controls it is given. If your systems are well-organized, with tight controls and robust security ensuring that AI accesses only designated data from trusted sources, you will likely be set up for success. Conversely, a lack of controls can exacerbate problems; for example, if everyone has unrestricted access and can modify all data, AI will simply worsen those issues. Additionally, you risk AI modifying or deleting your data. You want to ensure that AI only has access to perform the activities you *want* it to perform.

The absence of governance can lead to significant chaos, particularly in financial reporting. Establishing good governance processes, procedures, documentation, and workflows will greatly enhance your operations. However, there is often contention regarding the ownership of governance processes, as different stakeholders wish to exert control over what affects them. This dynamic has existed for a long time and will likely continue. Ultimately, leadership sets the policy, and each role within the process must be clearly defined. There should be opportunities for cross-functional input to foster accountability.

To ensure successful governance, focus on three key elements:

1. Security
2. Access
3. Oversight

Regarding access, it's crucial to have the right controls in place, maintain audit trails, and establish escalation paths for necessary changes. For oversight, ensure that proper processes exist, such as change management procedures and notification protocols, so that the relevant people and teams are informed of any changes before they encounter issues, like discovering that their usual database has shifted locations.

Defining access and establishing security procedures is essential. This means outlining who has access to and who owns each system. Furthermore, oversight mechanisms must be in place to ensure that all stakeholders can provide input and are notified of important changes.

To cultivate a successful governance function, form a governance committee, assigning seats based on the stakeholders affected by changes. For instance, if updates occur in your CRM, include representatives from marketing, finance, and IT on the committee. This way, as changes and updates take place, the right people are informed in advance, approvals are secured when necessary, and everyone impacted is notified and prepared for impending changes.

Additionally, it is vital to establish AI-specific guardrails defining who is responsible for training the models and who approves the outputs. There should be strict guidelines to prevent AI from generating outputs that violate legal standards or company policies or do not meet the expectations set by the governance committee.

I worked with a large bank that decided to implement AI in its mortgage application process. It fed a large dataset into the AI to train it on which mortgages had a high risk of default vs. those with an acceptable risk of default. They essentially built a "black box" in which the AI could use whatever correlations it made to determine which applications exceeded the risk tolerance threshold.

It turned out that the AI determined there was a correlation between the zip code of the applicant and the probability of default. It then started denying mortgage applications from anyone who lived in that zip code. This ended up being a violation of the law because that zip code was predominantly occupied by members of a protected race. Remember, we can have good intentions for a project but end up with outcomes that violate laws or regulations.

It is your responsibility to ensure that AI initiatives have the right guardrails in place to adhere to all laws and regulations. It is crucial to ensure that your AI isn't a "black box," where it makes a decision without outputting how it did so. The last thing you want is to be accused of violating a law, with your response being, "I don't know *how* the AI reaches its conclusions, but I can assure you we are not violating any laws." Transparency is key, which is why you want to implement your system with all this in mind from the start.

It's also crucial to ensure that AI understands the required standards, such as how to interpret response formats (e.g., recognizing "Y-E-S" for yes and "N-O" for no). It should follow specific naming conventions, whether they are in all capitals, lowercase, or proper case. Downstream systems see "YES," "Yes," "YeS," "Y," "True," "TRUE," and "T" as different things. Even though the difference between them may seem minor, it is easy for downstream processes to get tripped up if the wrong designation is used.

Below are some common governance gaps that organizations may encounter:

1. **Access:** It's possible for too many individuals to have admin or write access to data. For example, if a number in the database is changed and there is no record of who made the change or why, or if logging and auditing procedures are absent, identifying the source of the problem can be difficult. Therefore, implementing proper governance is essential to maintain data integrity and accountability.

2. **Approvals:** Whenever a change is made to the system, you want to have documentation showing that it was approved and that everyone was notified. It is also essential to have policies in place that restrict data changes to authorized individuals. Others with access to the data should only have read access or, if necessary, no access at all. Too often, changes are made, and everyone starts asking, "Who approved this?" or "When was this approved?"

3. **Audit tracking:** You should have audit capabilities that allow you to track what changed, when it changed, and who made the change. Other issues encountered relate to the metadata chapter, particularly concerning enterprise-wide standards for naming conventions and master data management. For instance, I once observed a CRM system that used free-form text for customer names, while an

ERP system employed different free-form text. Coca-Cola was recorded as "Coca-Cola" in one system and "The Coca-Cola Company" in another, leading to tangled data.

4. **Notifications:** Another gap arises when there is no change management process to ensure that new standards or changes in standards are consistently followed. If a standard changes but there is no notification process in place, relevant stakeholders may remain unaware of the change. It's important to have proper change management, notifications, and approval processes so that everyone is informed in a timely manner, allowing them to provide input.

5. **Documentation:** It's common for companies to lack documentation regarding standards, changes to standards, and new records. Documentation is frequently overlooked in many implementations, as companies rush to complete projects on time or within budget. This can lead to serious implications when documentation is needed later and cannot be found, or when a recurring error occurs without the initial fix documented. Unfortunately, when projects run over budget, companies often eliminate or reduce documentation time as a way to get back on track, as it is perceived as having low value. However, the effects of missing documentation often aren't noticed until it is too late. A colleague of mine had a client who was hit with ransomware. They lost access

to their financial budgeting and planning system and had to rebuild it from scratch. They had to pay the consultants to rebuild the application from scratch and reengineer the system, since they completely pulled documentation out of scope to stay on track in their implementation.

6. **Testing:** Another function that is often slimmed down from the scope is testing. I am often asked, "Do we really need to test all years in our application, or can we just test the last year and put that saved time toward our implementation?" It never seems like totally thorough checks are required when a project is starting to run over time or budget. The project goes live, but then, in year three, a small intricacy that was never tested causes downstream breakages. Also, brand-new implementations often get testing plans built. However, the organization overlooks testing policies and procedures for changes that happen after go-live. Everyone wants to build in a development environment, migrate to a test environment, and then deploy in production. Then they receive a request from a high-ranking executive that they need a piece of functionality *now*, and all policies and procedures seem to get bypassed to meet a deadline. Simple spot-checking replaces testing, and production gets deployed with a change that "I'm sure is fine!" until it isn't. Remember that standards are set from the top.

Promoting poor standards just to trigger a change when it's *convenient* for you can have ripple effects when anyone else *wants* the same.

A lack of transparency often characterizes processes for creating new accounts, updating records, or deleting records. When no one knows these processes, troubleshooting becomes challenging. Questions like "How did this happen?" "Who approved it?" and "When was it done?" cannot be easily answered. Consequently, organizations find themselves in a reactionary mode, addressing issues and errors arising from poor standards instead of taking proactive measures to prevent them.

I once worked with a large global bank that faced significant consequences from a government audit due to a notable deficiency. This situation had serious implications; they needed to remediate the deficiency by a specific deadline, or they would lose the ability to issue dividends to shareholders, which could adversely impact their stock price.

Interestingly, the audit issue was not related to incorrect numbers or unethical practices; rather, it stemmed from inadequate documentation explaining how data traveled from its origin in their ERP system to their final financial reports, such as their 10-Ks and 10-Qs filed with the SEC. We spent many months documenting every calculation and tracking data transfers between systems.

Ultimately, the client spent hundreds of millions of dollars to rectify the issue, whereas maintaining consistent documentation throughout the process would have incurred only a fraction of that cost. Additionally, the client was in the process of implementing new systems while we were documenting the prior lineage. As a result, once we finished the deficiency remediation, we needed to start over using the new systems. We had to do all this by hand because the client deemed a data lineage tool too expensive.

In summary, many issues arise from inadequate governance processes or poorly executed governance measures. Most of these can be addressed before we start our AI implementation. The goal is to be proactive and not reactive. The more proactive we are, the better equipped we will be to tackle these issues. This will also give us more time to address the unforeseen issues that always seem to come up, no matter how prepared we are.

Let's discuss what companies should implement to enhance their governance capabilities. First, it's essential to establish data classification and access rules, along with review boards for the data itself. This means that everyone who has access to the data truly needs it and has the appropriate level of access. Not everyone should have comprehensive access; some may only need to read the data, while others may not require access at all. It's crucial to have the right rules in place to manage this.

Compliance is also vital, particularly for public companies. Organizations must adhere to all relevant laws and regulations. Implementing master data management systems can help ensure that everyone communicates using a common language regarding metadata, including descriptions, data dictionaries, valid values, procedures, KPIs, and formulas. All these references should be consolidated into one centralized location.

It's important to have a documented approval process as well. This process should clarify who to approach if a change is necessary, and it may involve multiple levels of approval. It's not enough to simply ask a manager for a change in the CRM; you must also notify other relevant parties, like IT and marketing, about the change, as it might affect them. Documentation is essential to incorporate this into standard operating procedures.

Establishing a governance committee ensures adequate representation from all affected business units. There's nothing more frustrating for finance, IT, marketing, or any other group than decisions being made without their input. Therefore, it's critical to include everyone in the process and ensure proper notification regarding upcoming changes. While not every member of a department needs to be on the committee, each department should be represented by someone who can disseminate information effectively.

When developing governance frameworks, it's important to strike a balance. Oversight should not be so burdensome that it hampers progress or innovation. For instance, requiring numerous approvals for a simple financial report can waste time and bog down the process. On the other hand, lacking adequate procedures can lead to chaos, where anyone can generate reports without justifying their need. Having a policy that allows for such unchecked freedom can be detrimental.

Therefore, finding a middle ground is crucial: create a balanced approach that is robust enough to mitigate risk while still allowing for adaptability and flexibility within the company. It is equally important to define a separate process in the event that a quick change needs to be implemented. If it's 11 a.m. and you notice a material error in the report that goes out to the board at 11:30, there needs to be some type of quick process that allows you to act without having to go through four hours of approvals and meetings.

Imagine walking from your current location to your front door and needing approval from someone for every single step. This would make the process so cumbersome that you might decide not to move at all. On the other hand, if there were no guidelines, anyone could make changes as they see fit, leading to chaos. Different people might implement conflicting changes, which would result in confusion and conflict over terminology and methods.

As you can see, it's crucial to have someone in charge who can provide oversight. However, it's a delicate balance: you want to avoid micromanaging every little step while also allowing people some autonomy. The goal is to provide freedom within certain boundaries or guidelines.

When organizations are asked what their most valuable asset or the secret to their success is, they often answer, "Our people!" However, many overlook the importance and value of the people side of implementations. In the next chapter, we will tackle the importance of bringing in the right people with the right skill sets for our organization's initiatives.

Chapter 9

People: The Human Side of AI

Previously, we discussed how people within various organizations have differing opinions about AI. Some are enthusiastic about its potential, while others may be skeptical due to issues like hallucinations or previous negative experiences. However, a crucial aspect of implementing AI that is often overlooked is the human element.

For any project's success, whether it involves AI or any other technology, obtaining internal buy-in from all stakeholders is essential. This means engaging in early conversations with your team to ensure that you have the right people with appropriate skill sets who are excited about the implementation and not apprehensive about its impact on their jobs.

Organizations often fail to involve the right people early in the process. If someone joins a project halfway through or at the end, they may miss vital context, leading to poor decision-making and ineffective planning, including communication and training. For instance, if certain training elements were covered at the beginning but later skipped, new team members might lack adequate training with them. It is impossible to eliminate the need for training during a project. Employees change jobs, and new employees join the team all the time. It's also more efficient to train fifty people at once rather than one person per week for fifty weeks.

It's important to ensure that the right people from various groups are involved. This includes not only IT team members but also representatives from the business side and, possibly, external consultants or other departments within your organization. It's easy to trust the salesperson when they say that the software is self-implementing, only to find that you must have your own server set up to perform one of the tasks you need done—and when you approach IT halfway through the project, you learn that they are maxed out on servers and need three months of lead time to purchase a new one.

Another frequent mistake is mismatching skill sets. Companies sometimes assume that someone will automatically excel in a new role if they have experience in a related area. For example, a database expert may not necessarily have the expertise required for implementing a vector database or a graph database. It can be a significant change, with different optimizations required to run efficiently. Just because you are great at managing relational databases, it doesn't mean that you know everything there is to know about all databases. It's essential to assign people with the appropriate skills to ensure the project meets its intended use case and is built with best practices in mind. You want to avoid situations where team members are required to learn on the job or rely on self-study without proper mentorship to guide them through potential challenges.

In our age of free information, many employees turn to online resources, such as Google and YouTube tutorials, for learning. While these can be valuable resources, it is crucial to remember that the concepts are often taught in siloed environments with specific use cases. A solution that works well in one context may become complex when applied to a different scenario. Often, these tutorials are designed to handle a single use case with a single user executing it. They are not designed or built to scale to five hundred users across your global organization.

While these tutorials can serve as guides for proving the concept or testing select use cases, they should not replace having an expert architect a solution that meets your current and future needs and scales to your user base. I've worked with companies of all sizes, and not everyone has the budget to hire consultants to implement a project. If you need to complete a project with internal resources, that's perfectly fine. Just know that the value of time and money saved by bringing in a consultant often more than covers the cost of hiring them.

If you plan to staff a project internally, ensure that you have the right people with the necessary skill sets. If there are skill gaps, it's vital to bring in mentors, consultants, or trainers to address these deficiencies. This will help you avoid approaching AI implementation as complete novices. Instead, you'll benefit from the skills and experiences that come from lessons learned on the job. If you are just exploring the capabilities of AI, lost time or money may not be as big a deal; however, if you have a strict timeline for implementing a particular solution, you want to move as fast as possible, which means avoiding as many foreseeable issues as possible.

I was involved in a project a few years ago where the implementation was successful. However, the client learned that an implementation is more than just the initial setup. While our tool saved the client many hours and hundreds of thousands of dollars annually, they had not trained a resource for ongoing support. As a result, though the system was effective, it was abandoned after our team left because there was no one to maintain and improve it over time.

To successfully embrace AI, several key practices should be implemented to ensure that your team is structured effectively and the project is culturally set up for success. The first step is to establish clear roles and responsibilities for each team member. It is also crucial to maintain regular communication among team members, which could include status updates and expectations regarding communication. Training opportunities should be provided, allowing team members to work hands-on with the system as it is being developed.

It's essential to avoid surprising team members with a grand unveiling at the end of the project; instead, maintain a continuous line of communication. If end users see the technology as it is being developed, they will feel part of the solution and are much more likely to adopt it when it is released. If they are brought in at the very end, they will not feel ownership over the system and will not be as engaged.

It is important to clarify what employees' roles will be after the AI system is implemented, alleviating any fears about job security. If an employee feels that the technology will replace their job, they are unlikely to be an advocate for the system. They may even try to stall or sabotage the implementation just to save their own job.

Clarifying roles involves more than just informing employees that they will have a job going forward. If you tell them that they will have a job, they will not believe you. They will believe that you are just trying to get them to give you any information needed to implement the project. Then you won't need them anymore, and they will be fired.

A better approach is to sit down with each employee and identify aspects of their job that they wish they didn't have to do (opportunities for automation) and which parts they would like to spend more time on. Perhaps they are interested in taking on elements of a next-level role. Having a written plan will reinforce that there truly is a job for the employee once the project is finished. This will encourage them to fully embrace AI to enhance both the company's performance and their own skill sets.

Support is another critical component that is often overlooked. Once the system is live, a solid support plan is necessary. This includes understanding how support will be structured and what service-level agreements (SLAs) should be established to ensure that production issues are resolved promptly. Attention should also be given to handling common, lower-priority issues in a reasonable timeframe.

Often, the focus is excessively placed on implementing the system, with insufficient planning for ongoing support. Support is often just tossed over the fence to IT. IT might be responsible for supporting the application, but they need to understand the business's expected turnaround times and distinguish between IT and business requests. In a reporting system, the business may own the process of making and troubleshooting reports, while IT owns the process of getting data into the system. Each team needs to make sure they have the right resources in place to support this. If the business wants 24/7 support, additional resources might need to be hired so that there can be support shifts.

Identifying the people responsible for maintaining the system is vital, as is ensuring that they possess the necessary skill sets. Engaging advisors or consultants can help fill any gaps in expertise. Many organizations are unaware that consulting firms can provide "managed service" support, which involves fractional support for an application. If your system doesn't need a full-time resource to manage or maintain it, it may be worth asking your preferred vendor if they offer managed service support. I have clients who sign up for as little as ten hours of support per month. It's much cheaper to buy a small block of hours than to hire a full-time employee.

In finance, the need for custom-coded solutions has increased. Therefore, finance teams are increasingly required to develop skills in key technologies like Python, SQL querying, and data extraction from relational databases, potentially including macros for basic coding. To enhance AI capabilities within an organization, consider establishing a center of excellence, creating a dedicated team, or outsourcing to stay informed about leading AI trends and required skills.

New advances in AI are happening every day, and it can be a job, in and of itself, to stay on top of current trends. Many companies, especially smaller ones, don't have the budget to have machine learning and AI resources on staff. In cases like these, it may be more advantageous to have a small managed service agreement in place with an outside company, to stay on the latest trends and meet with you every so often.

Having the right people on projects and providing effective training cannot be overstated; doing so allows for faster progress with fewer mistakes. Many details that are overlooked initially can become significant later. Proper system design from the beginning not only boosts project success but also enhances team confidence in the solution.

Nothing is more demoralizing than having to start over repeatedly before finally completing a project. Avoiding unnecessary setbacks can significantly improve employee morale. By the time the software is released, the employees won't even believe that it will work. This is why we want experts involved from the start. When stakeholders see a project running fairly smoothly, they are more likely to share the exciting new tools with others.

I'm often asked, "What are the top skill sets required for an AI implementation?" The answer may vary from organization to organization, but I can go over some of the core skills that are universal to any project. The most important skill sets for teams using AI include curiosity and a proactive attitude toward learning new trends and techniques related to data. As I mentioned before, AI is constantly changing, and the skills required to be successful today may not be the ones required to be successful tomorrow. However, if you're willing to research and stay on top of trends, you will have an advantage over competitors who do not.

To effectively work with data, it's important to feel comfortable with data retrieval, querying, and transformations. You should be open to adopting new methodologies and have a foundational understanding of basic AI concepts. There are many terms and concepts in this field, particularly concerning the various types of machine learning, such as regression analysis, random forests, time series analysis, and Monte Carlo simulations. If reading these terms sounds like you are reading hieroglyphics, you may want to invest some time into learning what these terms are at a high level, or at least speaking with someone who has a high-level understanding of these terms.

It's essential to know which tools and algorithms to use in specific situations. Along with this, there are various technical components to consider, such as vector stores and programming languages. Python, for example, is a powerful language frequently used in AI development.

You must be able to access your data and understand how to pull it effectively to support your AI initiatives. This involves knowing SQL for relational databases, understanding the structure of your data, and continuously working to improve and optimize the quality of your data throughout the process.

In the next chapter, we will focus on the AI implementation itself. Assuming you've completed the setup, we will walk through the key elements required for a successful AI implementation and the things to watch out for during design and implementation.

Chapter 10

Implementation Plans and Strategies

When companies hire me to begin their AI implementation, financial planning, or reporting initiatives, there are two common approaches.

CRAWL WALK RUN FLY

The first is to start small. This involves identifying a pain point that, while it may not be the most significant issue the company faces, can be addressed quickly for an easy win. In this method, we define a small project scope, establish success metrics, and implement a feedback loop. This is often referred to as the "crawl, walk, run, fly" method. The goal is to avoid taking on a project that is too large and moving too quickly, instead allowing the company to build its capabilities over time and gradually work toward more significant initiatives.

The second approach focuses on addressing the company's biggest pain point first. This method aims for the highest possible reward but comes with increased risk. It is essential to assess whether the team has the capability to implement a solution that tackles this major issue. Can the team take ownership of the project, including its maintenance, as discussed in the previous chapters? Often, teams lack the necessary skill set to solve a large problem immediately and may need to build up to it. This is why starting with this approach is riskier than the first approach.

I typically recommend starting with small, targeted pilots, proofs of concept, or minimum viable products (MVPs). This approach helps develop the team's skills to the point where they can tackle larger challenges. It's important to recognize that companies vary in their maturity levels, with some having teams ready to handle significant problems right away.

I tailor my approach based on several factors:

- The size of the company
- The magnitude of the pain points being addressed
- The existing skill set of the team

- The team's ability to maintain the solution once implementation is complete

All these aspects must be considered, along with additional factors from our assessment, which we discussed earlier in this book. Even if a team possesses the skills to take on big challenges, a lack of technology platforms to support the project can be detrimental. Every company is at a different stage of maturity and readiness for AI. Therefore, the best strategy is the one closely aligned to each company's maturity, capabilities, and skill sets.

This is why a thorough assessment is crucial. Understanding your company's position in its overall AI journey will clarify what use cases to prioritize. More often than not, we start with small, quick wins before tackling larger challenges. However, securing a significant win can rally the entire company behind it and generate support for future projects.

We aim to balance the expected outcome, associated risks, and the overall probability of success, not only from an implementation perspective but also regarding ongoing maintenance. It's important to consider how to achieve the best buy-in from the team involved in the project, as well as from executives who will decide on budget approvals and project initiation. If executives are looking for a substantial win, we need to account for that while aligning with the project's goals.

If a big win is the goal but we don't yet have the necessary skill sets or technology platforms, we need to present our best case and explain why we recommend starting small rather than targeting the biggest pain points first. There are pros and cons to both approaches, and it's important to align our recommended strategy with the capabilities of our team, the technology available, and the data we've assessed.

If we are mandated to get the job done anyway, we can develop a strategy to mitigate the risks associated with skill sets and technology platforms. Perhaps we set up a new cloud environment to get the project up and running quickly. Then we can integrate it with our on-premises infrastructure. We can mitigate the skill set gap by hiring experienced consultants to run our implementation and provide managed service support while our team ramps up on the knowledge required to take over maintenance a few months after go-live. There are always adjustments we can make to mitigate risks; the earlier we can identify the risks, the more options we have.

When deciding where to start, we first identify if there's an urgent problem that needs immediate attention. For instance, is there a high-priority issue that could lead to trouble if not addressed soon? We also need to consider sponsorship. Can we secure the budget needed to complete the project? Will starting small increase our chances of obtaining approval, or is it more feasible to request a larger budget upfront?

When assessing potential projects, we must evaluate the odds of success. For example, would it be easier to gain funding for a $100,000 project with a seventy-five percent chance of success or for a $5 million project with only a five percent chance?

I often receive questions about how to identify urgent problems within a company. A good starting point is to analyze where most of the work is concentrated. Are there employees overwhelmed by manual tasks? For instance, if it takes four hundred hours a month to create an executive financial presentation, we should examine the specific tasks involved. Even reducing the time required by half could constitute a significant win.

Additionally, it's important to balance the time saved against the cost of these tasks and their frequency. Reducing two hundred hours in a monthly report is far more impactful than cutting the same amount from a report that is generated only every six months or so. Therefore, we should evaluate the volume of manual work relative to how often those tasks occur, alongside the overall benefits of streamlining those processes.

When it comes to AI, it's easy to get caught up in the technicalities of how it functions and what platforms are necessary for rapid automation. Before implementing extensive AI capabilities, learn the fundamentals of AI. Start by understanding how to effectively communicate with, or prompt an AI system. Numerous free tools are available where you can input a sample data set, pose questions, or issue commands to explore how to achieve at least a baseline level of success by manually providing data for insights or analysis.

Once you become comfortable prompting the AI and understand how to communicate with it effectively to achieve a reasonable level of accuracy, you can start focusing on the information required to prevent hallucinations. This includes exploring ways to obtain more accurate and faster results and considering how to manually address these issues. Eventually, you can explore automated methods to ensure that the AI receives the relevant information necessary to provide the desired outcomes.

When implementing AI or any type of technology, it's essential to have a strong foundation. The key building blocks for successful implementation may vary depending on the technology, but without the right foundation, the whole implementation could collapse.

One of the critical aspects to begin with is defining clear goals. Ask yourself, "What do we hope to achieve with this implementation? How will it benefit us? What does it mean in terms of cost savings, time savings, and possibly new capabilities that we didn't have before?" You must also have clean inputs, returning to the importance of data accuracy. Engaging the right stakeholders and establishing a feedback loop to keep everyone informed is vital.

```
   ┌─────────────────────┐
   │      FEEDBACK        │
   │       LOOP           │
   ├─────────────────────┤
   │      CONTEXT         │
   ├─────────────────────┤
   │     KNOWLEDGE        │
   │       BASE           │
   └─────────────────────┘
```

BUILDING BLOCKS OF AI SYSTEMS

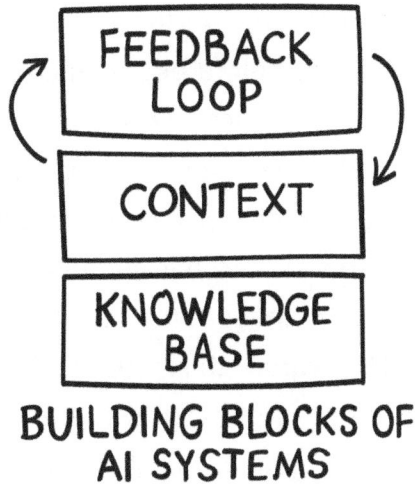

AI implementation has three main building blocks. The first, and foundational, element is the knowledge base. The second layer consists of the prompt or context provided to the AI. Finally, the third component is the feedback loop that ensures that the system improves in accuracy over time.

So, what do these individual components entail? The knowledge base is the collection of information fed to the AI to ensure accurate results. For instance, if an HR department creates a chatbot to answer questions about expense policies, the chatbot's effectiveness depends on the information it has received. If you were to ask the chatbot, "Is my airfare to a training course reimbursable?" the AI might generate an answer based solely on its general training data, which could lead to inaccuracies, what we call "hallucinations."

However, if you were to provide the AI with your company's complete expense policy before posing the question, it would know precisely which expenses are allowed, which aren't, the thresholds that need to be met, and the required approval levels. As a result, the chatbot could accurately respond, informing you that your airfare is reimbursable, but you need to discuss it with your manager and have them send an email confirmation to HR within thirty days of submitting the receipt. This response is significantly more accurate than the one you will get from a general AI platform that doesn't have access to your company's specific policy.

Thus, establishing a strong knowledge base involves implementing data, metadata, and technological components. It's important to ensure that you have clean, accurate data that can be used to achieve the right outcomes. You should also have appropriate metadata to point to relevant data and be on a scalable platform that can support the data and application layers needed for your solution. These elements are crucial in determining the quality of the knowledge base.

To illustrate these points, consider the following example: We have a transaction table in our data warehouse that contains our income statement. It may have some sample rows that look like this:

Account	Month	Year	Amount
Sales	Jan	FY25	500
Cost	Jan	FY25	250

I can ask my AI system to generate an SQL statement that shows my net income for January 2025, but how would it know where to go to get the information to answer my question? What database is it connecting to? What schema is it connecting to? What table(s) is the data stored in? What columns are needed in the resulting data set? What do I need to filter out in my resulting data set? What are the valid values I can choose from in my filters to get the right answer?

These are just a few of the questions that a person or AI would have when presented with that question. This is why it is important to have data dictionaries in place to help guide the AI. If I ask the question without providing the AI with the necessary knowledge, it will generate an answer based on its training data. It will give me an SQL statement back, but it will be entirely made up and not applicable to our environment. It will guess the answers to each of the questions it has, and its assumptions will not be correct.

Let's look at a better way of asking the AI. Suppose we feed it some summary information, such as the database name, the schema we are pulling the data from, and the name of the table we are pulling the data from. The AI will be able to give us a better answer than before; however, it will still guess the names of the columns and the values to filter on. Although our accuracy has improved, with a higher percentage of answers correct, we still won't reach the correct answer.

Next, let's feed the AI the names of the columns and the data types associated with each of those columns. It now knows that we have four columns: Account, Month, Year, and Amount. It knows that Account is a text column, Month is a three-character text column, Year is a four-character text column, and Amount is a number. The AI will now be able to infer that we want the Account and Amount columns to show our net income. It will be able to guess that the month will be designated by the three-character month (Jan, Feb, Mar) but won't know if the month is designated as "Jan, Feb, Mar," "JAN, FEB, MAR," or "jan, feb, mar." It will know that the year is a four-character text but won't know if it is designated as "2025," "FY25," or "fy25." It knows that Account is a free-form text input, but it won't know if I have an entry in there called "Net Income" or if it has to be calculated based on the data in there.

As you can see, we are getting progressively more accurate as we feed more information into the AI system. To complete this exercise, we can also pass text descriptions and valid values for each of the fields so that the AI has almost everything it needs to answer the question. It now knows *where* it needs to go to answer the question. It knows what columns it needs to pull.

However, now that it knows the sample values for the month, it knows that the month should be designated in the proper case. It now knows that the year is designated as "FY" followed by the two-digit year. Now, the AI knows the filter criteria required for *month* and *year,* so it can easily perform this piece. It will look through the valid Accounts, notice that there is no "net income" member, and will perform a calculation based on what it understands "Net Income" to be. If you want a fully accurate answer, ensure your knowledge base includes the math required to calculate "Net Income." Once you feed this into the AI, it will return a proper SQL statement with the right calculation over the right period of time.

The second building block is the prompt or context provided to the AI. Crafting effective prompts requires understanding both how to prompt AI and what key components make an effective prompt. Before jumping into what elements need to be in place for a good AI prompt, let's talk about the importance of effective prompts.

Many elementary school children go through an exercise about giving instructions. In third grade, my class was asked to create a set of instructions on how to brush your teeth. One student would say, "Open the toothpaste," and the teacher would find a creative way to try to open the toothpaste, maybe by taking a pair of scissors and trying to cut open the tube. Then the student would correct themselves and tell the teacher to unscrew the top of the tube. The teacher would grab the top and turn it the wrong way, prompting the student to correct themselves and then ask the teacher to turn the cap counterclockwise to unscrew the top. This exercise would go on and on until the teacher brushed his or her teeth.

While this may seem like a silly exercise, it is important to understand that working with AI is a similar process. When you give the AI precise instructions, it will perform the task with a high degree of accuracy. When you leave out details in the instructions, the AI will fill in the missing pieces with assumptions based on its training data. This may or may not lead to inaccuracies.

Here's an example: suppose we ask the AI to generate an input form for us with three input boxes and a "Submit" button on a web page. We may get something like this:

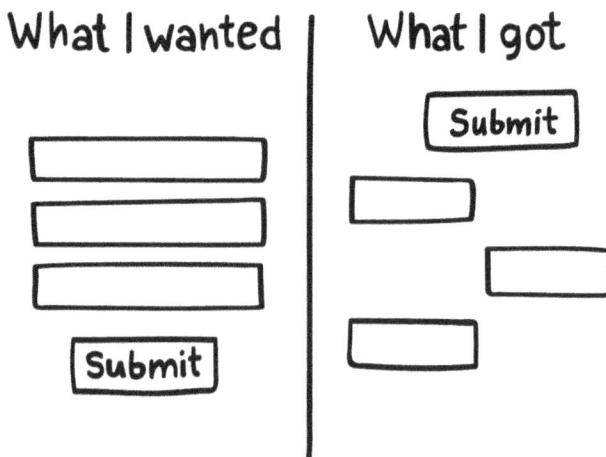

We may look at this output and think that the AI is bad and doesn't know what it is doing. The reality is that you didn't specify all the requirements you had, and AI filled in the gaps with its own assumptions. What you received wasn't wrong... you received a web page with three input boxes and a submit button. However, visually, it doesn't look professional. Had you specified that you needed a web form with three input boxes, each centered and aligned one under the other, with a submit button centered and aligned under the three input boxes, your results might have been a lot more accurate.

It can often be easy to overlook some of the simplest instructions. Our minds make assumptions about what should go without saying, and we assume that the AI knows what we mean. However, AI interprets our request in a different way, causing a response that is different from what we expect.

Based on experience, one fundamental tip is to always assign a specific role to the AI when prompting it. For instance, to effectively analyze data, it's important to specify, *"You are an expert data analyst."* When you indicate the persona or role that the AI should adopt based on the specific task, you are more likely to receive accurate answers than if you were to simply ask a question without context.

It's essential to clearly articulate the question you want to ask and avoid leaving room for interpretation. For instance, we looked at the example where we asked AI to create a grocery shopping list. It didn't know it was creating a list for a vegan and made one that included meat, eggs, and fish. We want to ensure that we are prompting the AI with a good question that includes all the required information to receive an accurate response.

Part of creating a good prompt involves supplying the correct data from your knowledge base to answer the question. It's worth noting that the formatting of your prompt can significantly affect its effectiveness. A plain text prompt may yield a certain level of accuracy, but using formats like Markdown, where you can incorporate headers, bullet points, and examples, can greatly enhance clarity and accuracy. Creating a prompt in Markdown format can help emphasize key portions of the prompt and even provide the AI with a step-by-step approach to solving the problem, ensuring that the AI goes through all steps required to get to the answer, rather than just jumping to an answer from the start.

If you're asking the AI to perform a calculation, providing the formula along with specific values and expected outcomes can lead to better results. For instance, if you say, "A plus B equals C" and then add, "Let's say A is 1 and B is 1, so C should equal 2. Now tell me what C is when A is 2 and B is 6," this gives the AI clear context rather than merely presenting the formula and expecting understanding.

The more information and context you provide, the higher the probability of receiving an accurate response. You may be asking questions like, "What is the right number of examples to provide the prompt?" This is more of an art than a science. I like to look at the equation that I am providing and ensure I am giving at least one example of every permutation of the answer.

If I am asking a question that involves logic *("If A, then do this, if B then do that, if C, then do that"),* then I like to make sure I have an example that covers each path as well as a negative test *("Assume A, then do this. Assume B, then do that. Assume C, then do that. Assume D, then return 0").* This leaves no room for interpretation; the AI knows what to do if one of the anticipated responses is provided, as well as an incorrect response. You'd be surprised by how many people try to trick the system when the key is accounting for all possibilities, so you don't get adverse results.

An obvious but little-known tip is that if you feel your prompt could be improved but are unsure how, you can ask the AI for assistance. Simply present your prompt and ask, *"Can you optimize this for me?"* or *"What might be missing that could lead to misunderstandings?"* Doing so can yield valuable insights that improve your prompt's effectiveness. You can also provide the AI with the prompt and ask, *"Based on this prompt, I entered A, and I got [XYZ] as my answer. How can I tweak my prompt so that I get [this] instead of [XYZ]?"*

Now that we've talked through the key elements of the prompt, let's look at the final building block of an effective AI system: implementing a feedback loop. This is essential for creating a system that becomes more accurate over time through continuous use. While one-off questions may not require this feedback mechanism, if you want the AI to learn from mistakes and successes, the feedback loop is vital. This could be as simple as caching results from specific questions or allowing users to rate answers with a thumbs-up or thumbs-down. Users might also provide feedback that the system can interpret to refine its algorithms.

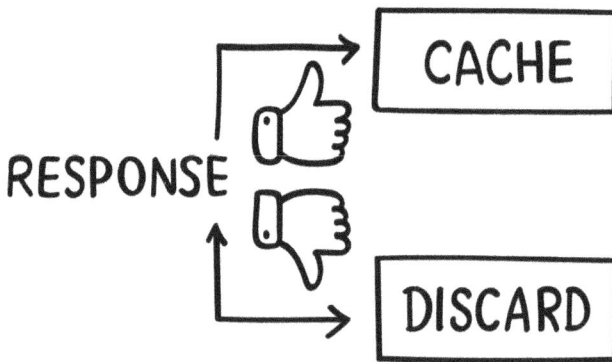

In the diagram above, we implemented a simple feedback loop into our application. We introduced a cache, where similar questions can be retrieved from memory rather than having the AI reprocess the request. The idea here is that if I ask what my net income was for January FY25 and the AI responds with $250, I can mark this answer as either correct or incorrect. If I mark it as correct, it now gets stored in a cache.

If I ask the same question a month from now, the answer should not change unless a reclassification has happened. Instead of going through all the processing that a language model may require, I can have the answer instantaneously pulled from the cache with the $250 response returned. This saves the processing power that the AI model requires. It also saves money since most hosted LLMs will charge based on the prompt size.

Providing the AI with the question, the relevant knowledge base entries, the right context, and examples can require a large prompt size. If many of these requests arise, it can lead to a high cost. By caching the responses, we can bypass the LLM processing, which will skip that cost. If the system cannot find the answer in the cache, it indicates that the question is new and will be processed by the LLM to obtain a response. If a user marks the answer as wrong, it doesn't get cached, so the LLM will process it again.

This is a very simple caching process. You can even expand it to feed the wrong answers back to the prompt so that it knows what answers to avoid. Be cautious when using this approach, as feeding too many incorrect answers can cause confusion and lead to additional errors.

We want to enable the AI to identify what it does correctly and what it needs to improve. Establishing this kind of system ensures that the AI learns from experiences, improving its accuracy over time. It's important to track success continuously rather than waiting until the end of a project to evaluate whether the implementation was successful.

To identify opportunities for improvement, it is essential to monitor each step of our process. We should ask ourselves if there are ways to enhance this particular process and measure its effectiveness. This approach will help us make our overall operations more efficient and accurate over time, ultimately improving the quality of our results. After all, the last thing we want is to invest millions in an implementation only to discover that its accuracy is only fifteen percent.

As we step through our process, we need to track and measure our performance. Are we improving? Are we approaching our end goals? It's crucial to align our efforts with the vision of the implementation, instead of merely hoping for a successful outcome after completing the project. Another question we can ask ourselves is whether there is a feedback system at each step that, if implemented, can improve the accuracy of our overall project.

We should not wait until the end of the project to find out what is feasible. Instead, we need to establish small, measurable milestones along the way. This strategy will allow us to validate the concept early, create a minimum MVP, and subsequently develop a production-ready system, ensuring that we are informed early on if certain objectives cannot be met.

Asking key stakeholders for buy-in, budget increases, or additional resources is often necessary. By providing them with confidence that we will fulfill our mission and reach our goals, we build trust and support. Additionally, we should incorporate natural checkpoints to monitor the project's health throughout its duration.

We should never pass a deadline without realizing it; we want to know as early as possible whether we are on track or if the deadline is at risk. Understanding the feasibility of the project is crucial. The more data we gather and analyze, the better equipped we will be to make informed decisions: Should we continue with the project? Should we abandon it? Do we need to adjust the project scope?

Lastly, it's important not to be overly concerned about the system's accuracy at the beginning. The goal is to improve over time by continuously refining the prompts, knowledge base, and supporting information. Instead of aiming for ninety percent accuracy during the proof of concept, the focus should be on validating the concept itself. Once that is achieved, we can implement components to enhance accuracy and repeatability in our processes.

Common mistakes companies make during the implementation phase include a lack of preparation and failing to recognize early on that a task may not be feasible or that the necessary information to proceed was not provided. Additionally, unclear metrics for defining project success can hinder the company's ability to know if it has met its goals. Skipping change management procedures can leave end-users and stakeholders uninformed about progress, and not setting clear expectations can lead to confusion about roles moving forward. Sometimes, ownership can become siloed, with certain processes viewed as purely IT concerns when they actually require collaboration between IT and the business.

Another common mistake is blindly trusting the output of an AI system. Too often, organizations build an AI to generate an SQL statement and then have a process execute that SQL statement. What if the SQL statement created is wrong? What if it deletes data instead of reading it? Blindly trusting the AI to perform the right action one hundred percent of the time can be a big mistake.

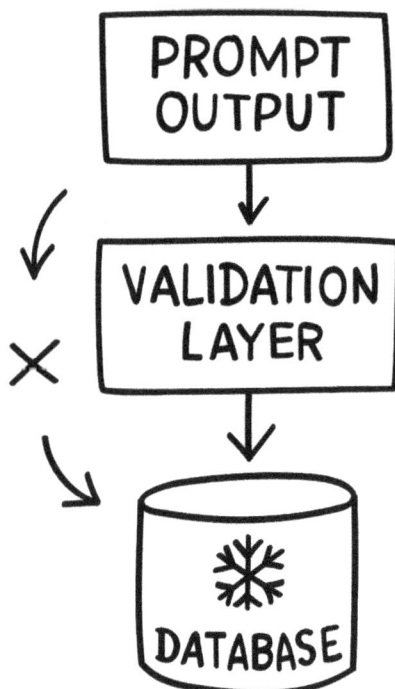

Instead, we want to ensure that there is a validation layer between the outputted database query and the execution of that query so that we are running basic checks, such as correct syntax, correct query operation (select vs. delete vs. update), and correct security provisioning.

You might say, "We set up the security on the AI user so it can't delete data. Do we still need a validation layer?" The answer is yes, you do. Processes break down all the time, resulting in a lag between when security needs to be provisioned and when it is actually provisioned. Sometimes, security gets accidentally deleted or copied from one user to another. We don't want a mistake in security provisioning to allow the AI to wipe out all your data.

The same can be said of programs and scripts. A common use case for AI in finance involves using AI to generate Python code for machine learning on the data. Perhaps, we are looking for correlations or to have the AI forecast data for the next six months.

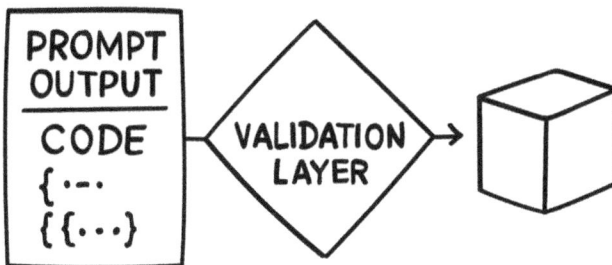

Just as with SQL, we never want to automatically trust code that is generated from an AI. Trusting code is more dangerous than trusting SQL. With SQL, you can potentially delete data in your database. Trusting Python code, however, could potentially cause massive issues, such as wiping out servers and networks, downloading viruses, etc. It's important that all code generated from an AI model be validated and then executed in a container that is destroyed after execution. You don't want AI writing code against your servers. If anything malicious finds its way in, your organization will be severely impacted.

There's a lot to consider when implementing AI for your organization. If I mentioned every possibility, you'd be looking at a book with thousands of pages. I hope that what I have covered has given you a glimpse into the complexity of implementing an AI project and some of the key considerations to think about *before* undertaking a new project. The good news is that AI technology is constantly evolving and becoming easier to implement. As new models emerge, staying on top of the latest trends is crucial to continually improving the accuracy and effectiveness of your solutions.

Chapter 11

Project Management and Post Go-Live

Many companies implement their systems and then ask, "What's next?" Hopefully, you aren't waiting until the end of the project to figure this out! Remember, everything should be done with the end state in mind. We want to look past our initial release to the next six to twelve months to see what "post go-live" looks like. Now, there will be some aspects that we can't envision before we start the project. These will be items that come up over the course of the implementation.

A few categories of requests may come up during project implementation: scope additions, scope subtractions, scope deferrals, and application enhancements. Project managers *love* to talk about scope. Scope, in case you are unfamiliar, is the set of tasks and activities committed to the project.

For example, if we are making a simple calculator with add/subtract capability in Excel, we are going to create an Excel document with two input cells, an operator cell, a submit button, and a results cell. Our scope includes the following objectives:

1. Create an Excel document.
2. Develop a method to input values into two cells.
3. Apply an operator (either addition or subtraction).
4. Display the result of the calculation.

Being able to multiply or divide the two numbers would be considered "out of scope" since it would not be functionality we want in our base product.

In the example above, let's say that we realized during the project that we need the ability to multiply the two numbers together. That was not part of our original scope, so we didn't design a process that allows for additional operators. The key question we want to ask ourselves is: *Is multiplication capability something we can't go live without, or can it wait until after the project ends?* The reason this question is important is that, during a project, once the team realizes the capabilities of the tool, their minds start to wander. *If the tool is so good at adding and subtracting, maybe it can multiply, too!* In their excitement, they decide to add it to scope.

It's the same concept with an AI tool; once you see its capabilities, you are going to be tempted to apply it everywhere.

You want to make sure you distinguish between a core feature that is required for the implementation and one that is an enhancement to layer in after the project is over. My rule of thumb is to track all new scope requests on a separate list. Each item is categorized as one of the following:

1. Must-have for go-live
2. Enhancement that can be implemented after go-live
3. New functionality that can be deferred to a future phase (not necessarily immediately after go-live)
4. Nice-to-have

It's important to remember that every time we add new scope to our project, we need to be willing to do one of the following:

1. Extend the project timeline, which also implies a budget increase.
2. Increase the project budget by bringing on additional team members to implement the new functionality without delaying deadlines.
3. Remove one or more items from the current scope to offset the change in time and/or cost.

Keep in mind that whenever you add new items to scope, requirements gathering, design, build, test, documentation, and deployment activities go with them. It's never a matter of just adding another button! You also have to plan for the button, the user interface for that button, the functionality behind the button, testing that the button does what it should, testing that the new functionality doesn't break existing functionality, ensuring the button scales to the user base that you will have, and the deployment of that button.

Key Tip: When a client asks me to add new scope, I never tell them no. Instead, I estimate the activities and time associated with those activities. I then ask them if they are okay with either shifting the deadline by [X] days, increasing the budget by $[Y], or removing other functionality from scope. You'd be surprised at how many times these "must-have" features become "deferred for future phase" items!

The reason I spent so much time talking about scope is that it is crucial to evaluate your project at the end based on its success. Evaluating scope changes is a good metric for looking at the project's success. It shouldn't be the only metric, but it is often ignored.

In the example above, let's assume that we budgeted one week and $1,000 to make our calculator. However, when we get to the implementation phase, the team realizes that creating the addition function was far more challenging than initially planned. It turns out that we will need a second week to build the subtraction function, which will cost us another $1,000 to implement. The manager of the project doesn't want to ask the steering committee for more money, so he decides to cut the subtraction function from scope. The result is that the project is completed in a week at a cost of $1,000.

Was this project a success? Technically, the project was delivered on time and on budget. However, when you look at the scope, not all project functionality was delivered by the deadline. This is why we want to look at time, budget, and scope for our project success metrics. We also want to look at time savings, cost savings, company capabilities, and team learning as other metrics to measure our ROI.

I've spent a good amount of time explaining scope because it is often overlooked when determining project success. Because of this, it is the easiest metric to manipulate in order to finish a project on time and on budget. By examining cost items and scope, I identified a $100 million cost overrun on a program I was auditing.

Beware of scope creep. Running over time or budget is rarely the result of one big change to scope. It is, instead, often the result of adding many smaller items to scope. That's why it's so important to manage scope. It's too easy to look at new functionality that "only takes a few days" and add it to scope. When you have a bunch of those enhancements, you can be adding weeks or even months to your project timeline.

We've discussed activities that may be unforeseen. Now let's talk about the activities we can foresee before our project begins. The first of these is support. While rarely considered at the beginning of a project, it is critical to at least have a basic framework in mind prior to project initiation.

What does the support model look like? Are you relying on IT to own and service everything, or are there aspects of the implementation that your team is supporting? It's easy to throw all support activities over the fence to IT, but remember that we don't want to wait for the end of the project to start ramping up the support resource. Make sure you have time baked into your project plan for the support resource(s) to see the application prior to its release. It's also easy to assume that there will be plenty of time for training. Many projects that run behind have documentation, training, or testing reduced from scope to stay on track. All those training sessions you envisioned end up becoming a single session packed with a ton of brand-new information, all crammed into a half-day.

Does your support team have the skill set required to support the application after go-live? Many companies try to save money by asking someone with little to no experience to learn the new tool. While this can save money in the short run, it may be more expensive long term. You may be sacrificing responsiveness to major issues.

I once worked with a company where the support staff accidentally deleted core components of the application because they hit the wrong button. Why didn't they just look back at the documentation and recreate it? It turned out that they eliminated the documentation from scope to save two weeks on the project timeline. Luckily, I had some offline backups and was able to revert the change.

Sometimes, a team member is trained up because the support required does not warrant hiring a full-time employee. The risk added by having an inexperienced support staff can be substantial. I've seen successful projects get canceled after go-live because the support team couldn't adequately manage the system.

As mentioned earlier in the book, many consulting firms offer "managed services," where they can offer fractional support staff in the event that you need support for your application but don't require a full-time resource. Many vendors have minimum hour requirements for their support contracts, with lower costs offered if you guarantee more hours per month. My company offers managed services with minimums as little as one hour per month.

Another important support component is the service-level agreement (SLA). The SLA defines how responsive your support team will be for the application. Everybody wants instant support, offered exactly when they reach out. However, the support for your systems should match the type of system being supported. For example, a mission-critical system needs to have a very tight SLA, while a less important application can have a looser SLA.

SLAs typically call out the following metrics: response time and average time to resolution. SLAs may also have tiers, depending on the type of issue. The response time indicates how long it takes for you to get a response after you issue a support request. For example, many organizations have high, medium, or low priority as options for the support request. A low-priority request might have an eight-hour response time, whereas a high-priority request might have a one-hour response time. Remember, this is the time it takes for the support request to be acknowledged. It is rare that the issue will be resolved within the one-hour window.

The next metric is the target time to issue resolution. A low-priority request may have a few-day target, with a high-priority request having a one-day or less target. Remember that if you have a mission-critical system that requires a high degree of uptime, a high-priority request may target resolution in a few hours rather than in a day.

Keep in mind that not all issues are fixable within the target resolution time. For an issue requiring a code change to the application, time is needed to identify the issue, debug it, resolve it, test it, and then deploy the change. Depending on the change, additional regression testing may be required to ensure that the fix did not break something else along the way.

It is not always practical to have one hundred percent of issues resolved within the target window. Wherever possible, you should bake in time to build automated tests. This is a great investment in the long-term health of your project. Future patches/releases, as well as bug fixes, can save a lot of time by automating tests instead of relying on manual human testing.

If you purchase a software product from a vendor, it will most likely include a maintenance window during which application downtime may occur. This downtime can be for installing patches to the system or for any maintenance that needs to happen to the underlying servers. Many vendors will allow you to choose what the maintenance window is for your organization. Be sure to choose a time that is least intrusive to your team. Having your team in one or a few time zones may be easy to plan around; having a global team will require scheduling downtime during productive hours for some team members.

Having a service-level agreement in place is more than just a promise to address issues within an agreed-upon window. Be sure to review any contracts with vendors to see what the consequences are for missed SLA windows. If the result is merely an apology, there is no real incentive for the vendor to address issues within the agreed-upon timeframe, and you will need to set your team's expectations accordingly.

It's important to negotiate incentives for the vendor to meet their SLA times. Maybe there is a refund required for all missed responses and resolution times. Now your vendor has a reason to meet all SLAs, which will improve the quality of your service. If your support team is internal, it may be challenging to implement similar incentives for support, unless part of their compensation is tied to meeting SLAs. If there is any incentive for SLAs, make sure you are tracking the metrics rather than relying on the vendor's reporting for SLAs. Vendors with the ability to hide certain support instances may be falsely reporting their results.

Enhancements are another foreseeable part of your project timeline. *What* enhancements end up on the enhancement list will vary over the course of the project. However, you can control *how* you will handle enhancement tracking and implementation. Some companies jump right into an enhancement phase right after the project is implemented. Others pause for a period of time after a project is implemented to collect user feedback and then enter into a formal enhancement phase. There's not necessarily a right answer here, but I recommend tracking the importance of each enhancement logged during project implementation to determine if it is needed immediately after the implementation or if its release is flexible.

Remember that technology is always evolving, so you shouldn't plan for a one-time implementation. Implementing a system that never changes will lead to many missed opportunities. Your go-live plans should include cycles of improvement and expansion of the technology across your company, where applicable.

Conclusion

I want to thank you for purchasing this book and reading it thoroughly. As I mentioned before, various resources on AI are available, so I appreciate your choice to explore this book for some of your answers.

We are at a very exciting time in AI, with numerous possibilities and capabilities being introduced every day. It's easy to fall behind and miss out on some of the exciting functionalities that are continuously being developed. We invite you to reach out to us for a conversation about your organization's current situation and what you might need to succeed moving forward.

As mentioned, there are many considerations to keep in mind before starting any project. This includes the initial implementation phase, during the implementation, and even after the implementation is complete. Staying updated on new possibilities and future capabilities, as well as maintaining your systems, is crucial.

Before you embark on your AI journey, make sure to conduct a thorough assessment, involve the right people early on, and consider reaching out to external resources, advisors, consultants, or coaches to enhance your chances of success.

Once again, I appreciate your thorough reading of this book and look forward to seeing where your AI journey leads you.

Additional Resources

I want to make sure you have every resource available for success. If you read through this book and need help determining if you are AI-ready, our expert team is ready to help you! As a special thank you for purchasing this book, we are offering a 50% off promotion:

You can also navigate here: https://masterfuldata.com/book-ai-ready.

I'd love to connect with you on my social channels. Below is a link to my Linktree, where you can find me on various social channels and websites!

https://linktr.ee/danvillani

Thank You For Reading My Book!

As a special thank you for reading this book,
we have provided a link for you to download our
Data Quality Checklist.

https://masterfuldata.com/book-dq-checklist

*I appreciate your interest in my book and value your
feedback, as it helps me improve future versions.
I would appreciate it if you could leave your invaluable review
on Amazon.com with your feedback. Thank you!*